The advice published in this book has been carefully compiled and reviewed by the author. However, a guarantee cannot be ensured. The contents of this book are for entertainment and information. The use of this information may be prohibited, depending on the jurisdiction. Check with your local authorities before playing.
Likewise, a liability of the author and his agents for personal, property or pecuniary damage is excluded.

„All success has its secret, all failures its reasons."
Joachim Kaiser, German critic

Michael Lutz

BLACK JACK

WITHOUT

BLACK OUT

The brilliant memory training for all card players

With numerous illustrations by the author

The German Library lists this publication
in the German National Bibliography

BLACK JACK

WITHOUT

BLACK OUT

The brilliant memory training for all card players

1st edition, in English, August 2024

Copyright © 2024 Michael Lutz, Bonn, Germany

ISBN: 978-3-759-71252-3

About the author

Michael Lutz has many years of experience as a freelance mental trainer with a focus on memory training (seminars, individual coaching, etc.) and energetic psychology (solving blockages in examination fears, stage fright, fear of flying, etc.). He is also a longtime lecturer at renowned institutes of adult education - e.g. Dr. Ebert Academy, Rhein Erft Academy, etc. - for adequate, practice-oriented training concepts using innovative memory strategies.

He has numerous publications among others in research and teaching, the professional journal of the German University Association, *Gehirn und Geist* (Brain and Spirit) and the publishing house *Spektrum der Wissenschaft* (Spectrum of Science).

His specialised field is solving blockades in golf, tennis, etc., including symptoms of tournament stress and the resulting impairment to motoric skills.

He is regularly present in the trade press and his seminars are highly rated.

Contact the author

If you have any questions or suggestions, especially regarding the translation - German < > English – or if you like to comment on my seminars or this self-study, please write to me:

Michael Lutz
Europaring 9
D-53123 Bonn

Lutz@genialgemerkt.de
www.genialgemerkt.de

A request in advance

Have you already attended one of my memory seminars or read one of my books?!
Then I would like to thank you once again at this point.
I constantly revise the content and exercises of my books, so that future seminar participants or readers get the greatest benefit from my projects.
I would be very happy, if you shared your personal impressions and suggestions with me for improvement.
Thank you in advance for your efforts.

If you like to book me for a company seminar or another event, prefer private lessons or have questions about the memory, please write to me at:
lutz@genialgemerkt.de

I also may revise your training and teaching materials to adapt them for memorising. For more information on mental training, visit my website at:
www.genialgemerkt.de

Until then, I wish you all the best.

Content – Chapter 1

Preface	9
Remember playing cards as a brain dumbbell	11
How you should "work" with this book	13
The royal class	15
How efficiently do you use your brain?	17
The memory techniques of the memory athletes	18
Skat is healthy!	21
Brain halves and personality	23
Hidden performance potential	24
Structuring the biological disk	26
Memorized playing cards, an experiment: Part 1	28
Memorized playing cards, an experiment: Part 2	32
Memorized playing cards, an experiment: Part 3	34
All keywords in the overview	54
The deeper meaning	57
Remember names made easy	57
Remember by location	61
If you have children	63
Theme area four-color card game	66
Color diamonds	69
Color hearts	75
Diamonds and hearts together	77
Spades and clubs together	78
Folders and positions	79
A zoo in the skyscraper	82
The first time	91
Remember all 32 cards in their order!	104
In the casino	109
Your apartment list (individual characteristics)	110
Orientation guide	116
Example Skat	124
MLS / System / A methode	126
MLS at Skat	129
If you play Bridge	129
Remember numbers quickly and permanently	134
A 50-digit number in a few minutes	135
Summary of all game card values...	141
...and game card pictures	142

Content – Chapter 1

Definitions of diamonds cards	143
Definitions of hearts cards	151
Definitions of spade cards	159
Definitions of clubs cards	167

Content – Chapter 2

Hand on heart ... or better on brain	176
Basic rules and basic strategy	177
Number pictures - List	180
Tables structure	181
Double your bet	182
How to memorize tables quickly	183
Double - Remember the total points	184
Summary - Double the game bet	188
Splitting - Splitting the game cards	189
Summary - Splits	197
Buy playing cards	198
Hard hand	199
Summary - Hard hand	204
Soft hand	205
Summary - Soft hand	204
Counting game cards	210
Counting game cards - Brain access	215
List for game card counting	216
The first 10 game cards - Example	217
Counting without numbers	216
How you benefit	223
Recommendation	225

Preface
(even for those who do not normally read them)

As a skat player, I have been looking for a book for a long time, which gives tips on how to better remember playing cards. Since I did not find any book, I finally wrote it myself.

The result "**Memorize playing cards in seconds**" - may be of particular interest to those of you who like to play skat, bridge, poker, doublehead, sheephead, or similar challenging card games; may it be to remember the already played cards as fast and efficiently as possible or to know which cards are still in play.

The book "BLACK JACK without BLACK OUT" was the result of numerous requests from my readers who want to perfect their poker or just the blackjack game. These games are not "only" about memorizing as many as possible of the already played cards etc., but also about retrieving complex matrix tables in the form of so-called "basic tables" from memory during the game, for a possibly high profitable usuage.

In order to give you a basic understanding of the relationship between brain and memory, this book contains the most important information and memory techniques from my book *"**Memorize playing cards in seconds**" in the first chapter.

In the second chapter, you expand your knowledge to memory techniques with regard to complicated matrix tables and "to memorize something different" by means of practical applications and exercises using the example of the blackjack game.

All in all, this self-study enables you to assume far more than the book title suggests!

At the end of the course, you will find that the technique you acquire here - with a few minor changes - can be a real asset to everyday life, work, school, and even your whole life. Later, you can use these memory techniques almost everywhere you used to rely on pen and paper.

In addition, you will soon realize that your memory is far better than you ever thought possible, and that there's currently enormous potential for you hiding in secrecy.

Because: →

*Memorize playing cards in seconds"
„Spielkarten merken in Sekunden" – ISBN 978-3-839-16765-6

**A good memory
is not just a matter of intelligence and talent, but
rather, the method of remembering something.**

You will be amazed at the fantastic memory achievements that you will be able to make using the memory strategies described here. Of course, despite best memory techniques you cannot do without the exercises, but do not worry: The exercises in this book have nothing remotely to do with the dust-dry exercises that you know, for example, from your school days.

On the contrary. You will find that learning with these unusual, exciting and amusing exercises can be really fun and enjoyable. While working with this book, you will have experiences of a special kind. Experiences that will trigger feelings of success and happiness for you and thus increase your self-confidence. At the same time you train your brain, which is far more important than most people want to admit. Almost everyone believes that the task of the "mind - organ" (brain) is first and foremost to be its memory (knowledge store) and at the same time - by the way - to control life - sustaining bodily functions and organic processes fully automatically.

Very few people are aware that their brain, with all the life experiences stored in it - be it in a positive or negative sense - represents their personality, which makes them (mentally) human and makes them appear as such.

**While you train your brain,
Promote your personality at the same time!**

Remember playing cards as a brain dumbbell

In a healthy and well-trained brain, the natural age-related "signs of wear and tear" can be more than compensated by the corresponding experience of life, and so it is not without reason that one says:

> In the youth you learn, in old age you understand!

Furthermore, according to the latest findings in brain research, it is known that new brain cells (neurons) are still forming even in old age, and that even dead neurons elsewhere can be replaced by new ones. So they are not, as they believed until recently, irretrievably lost after their one-time loss.

However, in the case of a completely untrained and hardly demanded brain, the mind becomes more and more exhausted like an unused muscle. How many people go to a fitness center two or three times a week to keep fit* and exercise their muscles?!

But hardly anyone thinks about training their minds, too, so that in Germany, according to the latest estimates, we will have to live continuously with about 2 million people suffering from dementia, i.e. those in need of care.

Not to mention the suffering of those affected and their loved ones, one should consider the immense economic damage caused by this kind of carelessness for the community.

Because your brain - and therefore your memory - is comparable to a muscle in terms of its performance, you should also train it the way you strengthen your muscles in the gym. For this you should best internalize the following sentence:

> What are 20.000 volts in my arms good for,
> when there is no light on at the top?!

---

* The approximately 100 billion cells of the human brain, with their mass of about 1500 grams just 2% of the total body mass of a normal human weight.
Nevertheless, in normal operation, the brain consumes about 20% of the energy that we consume, for example in the form of food.
These facts should also be rethought, especially if one or the other "kilo" brings too much on the scales.

What movement is to the body is thought to the brain.

Even learning this self-study is an excellent and efficient memory training. And the subsequent regular use of these special memory techniques should be pretty much the best thing you can do proactively against forgetfulness.
I wish you, dear readers, a lot of fun, lots of success and many "aha-experiences" with my self-study.
Discover the extraordinary memory you have!

Yours,
Michael Lutz

How you should "work" with this book

The notes in this chapter are intended to help you to work with this book and thus to make the training of your memory as efficient as possible.

Learning environment
Successful learning works best in a stress-free and enjoyable environment. One of my most important recommendations is that you set a learning environment for your project as beneficial as possible.
This is not just a place where you feel very comfortable (like in your favourite chair), but above all a place where you will not be disturbed while learning.
Create a relaxed atmosphere for our exercises, so that you can fully use your mental capacity.

Errors
Grant yourself mistakes!
Do not fret, if you do not immediately understand something, but instead enjoy the things you already understand and can use.

Maximum 30 minutes
If you want to transfer certain exercise sections into your long-term memory, you should only learn for a maximum of 30 minutes and then - after a short break - try to repeat what you have learned until then mentally or in writing.

Knowledge building
Work with this book as if you were building a house. Begin with your construction project with the cellar (first page) and finish your knowledge building with the roof (last page), and not vice versa!
Do not skip any chapters or exercise parts for convenience or because you may think they may be too light or too heavy for you!

Worthy to remember
Since almost all exercises are performed playfully and with a lot of imagination, at first you might find one or the other strange aspect.
But that is an essential part of this technique. Look forward to trying something completely new and you will see:
The more "remarkable" these things "seem" to you, the better you will remember them!

You decide

Always remember: you are doing a self-study, so decide for yourself how much time you will need for this course.

Of course, you can distribute all practical exercises and practice sections over several weeks or even months, as long as you do not spend too much time between the exercises and repeat what you have learned so far, at least mentally.

With one exception:

Be sure to read pages 29-55 - from one coffee cup* to the next - in one piece!

A real win

If you take all these points to heart, you will soon be amazed by your own memory.

*The above graphic (coffee cup) always appears, when you are prompted to act or it has the function of a pause sign.

The royal class

Learning and retaining digital information, such as numbers, formulas, vocabulary, names, etc., is particularly difficult for most people because they usually try to solve these tasks with the wrong brain regions.

Remembering playing cards among the "memory athletes" is, so to speak, the royal class, because a playing card, in contrast to a "simple" number, consists of at least two values because of the corresponding color!

But this also means that if you have mastered a technique with which you can memorize the order of the playing cards of several card games, you will hardly have any difficulties to remember a 50-digit number, a long shopping list, names or other complex things.

As a result, this self-study course also contains numerous examples and practical exercises on these subjects.

Why is it difficult to remember playing cards?

The reason for bad card memory is the lack of efficiency with which we usually use our miracle brain!

Hardly anyone worries about which fantastic processes occur in seemingly lapidary, everyday situations in his brain.

For example, if I ask you the question, "Do you know who the middleweight boxing champion was in 1932?" You can answer that question in a fraction of a second with "yes" or "no."

Despite the unimaginable amount of data stored in your brain, you will not have the slightest trouble matching that data (all your knowledge) in fractions of a second to answer my question with an absolutely certain "Yes" or "No"!

Or think about the power of your brain when you watch a movie that is shown at a length of 90 minutes with 20 pictures per second.

Quite apart from the setting of the film, your brain needs to process as many as 108,000 images in 90 minutes. By the way, you may also talk to your partner, nibble nutlets and drink your beer.

If this film was really good then even after half a year you will have no trouble telling someone the plot of the movie and you will sometimes be able to remember very detailed pictures.

I could give you a lot of similar examples of what incredible powers our brain is capable of and what amazing things happen automatically in our thinking machine every day, without us noticing or thinking about it.

Unfortunately, this would go beyond the scope of this, so I would like to restrict myself to the circumstances relevant to our memory technique. Nevertheless, learning how to use our memory technique should at least essentially understand how the brain works, to understand the enormous capacities our brain already has and which capacities we have only partially or not yet used.

Knowledge gap thinking organ

Memory is derived from "memorise"!

Have you ever thought about it?

Most of us do not worry about the functioning of their mind and take it for granted that their brain is already functioning somehow. Just as we perceive the functions of our other organs, such as the heart, lungs, kidneys, etc. as a matter of course - at least as long as we are healthy.

If we then think about the connections between brain and memory, we usually want to answer these questions directly through our brains.

However, if we only want to understand the brain through our own brain, we quickly recognize our limitations!

How efficiently do you use your brain?

Let us compare your brain or memory with a car and its engine.

Imagine that you have never sat in a car before. So you have no idea of the possible acceleration and speed of a car.

Since you are not in the least interested in the technology of a car, you have absolutely no idea of the function or the performance and the mechanical structure of an engine.

For operational reasons, your employer will transfer you to another job. This is unfortunately much further away from your apartment than your old job, and you decide to buy a used car.

Somewhere you once heard that a car with a six-cylinder engine should be better than a car with a four-cylinder engine, and you buy the seemingly better. Since the car dealer is a nice person, he wants to quickly screw in some brand-new spark plugs in your "new" used cars. After he first removes the six old spark plugs and has already screwed in three new spark plugs, the phone rings in his workshop. In the phone call, the car dealer is told that he must urgently come to an accident with his tow truck. He interrupts his work on your car and drives to this accident site. If you want to pick up your vehicle at the car dealer on the agreed date, it has not yet returned, and so you get your car from an employee - who knows nothing of the three missing spark plugs - handed.

This story has been around for many years, and you still drive your old "six-cylinder car" with the three missing spark plugs. You may be surprised that sometimes a car can be seen on TV, which drives much faster than yours, even though it has only a six-cylinder engine and is even of the same type and manufacturer. But that does not bother you. The main thing is, you get to your job somehow, even if the vehicle on TV takes just a fraction of the time it takes your car to travel the same distance.

Rethink this comparison - brain/car - for a minute or two.

The memory techniques of the memory athletes

If you have not been preoccupied with memory techniques before this self-paced course, then this comparison (with the car) applies to you and to the efficiency with which you currently use your brain.

Many years ago, one failed to provide you with an instruction (the three missing spark plugs) for your brain, so you do not even know what enormous power your brain is capable of!

Surely you've seen a "memory artist" (the faster car of the same type) on TV or at an event that could easily remember a 200-digit number. Surely you have heard before that all these "memory acrobatics" use some strange techniques (spark plugs)?!

And yet you are deeply convinced that these people are absolute exceptional people and you would never even remotely be capable of such a thing!

Of course, such services require a high level of training and discipline; Nevertheless, all memory athletes in the world make use of memory techniques that can be learned and mastered by ordinary people.

Why not also from you?

A good memory is not only a matter of intelligence and training, but also of the method, the way I memorise something!

In other words, comparing the now-state of a normal and healthy brain with a car, I claim that each of us basically has a super-fast Formula 1 racing car.

Unfortunately, most of us spend the rest of their life chugged through the villages only in first or second gear, because very few are aware that their racing car (brain) also has a third, fourth, fifth and even sixth gear!

For explanation, I want to show you literally using a small two-part experiment.

Please close your eyes for a moment and try to visualize the following:

A hippopotamus!

I am sure that in no time you had a crystal-clear picture of this animal in your mind's eye.

Let us now turn to the second part of the experiment. Close your eyes again and try to visualize the following number as pictorially as possible:

Three million seven hundred eight and thirty thousand - two hundred eighty three!

If you're not exactly a synaesthetist, you probably had just a huge problem with your visual imagination! For your understanding, I would like to explain to you through the help of the following graphic.

*In synaesthetic experiences, visual, taste and acoustic sensations come together. Emotions, smells or flavors are visually perceived. Sometimes numbers, letters or sounds can be seen coloured.
Six out of seven synaesthetes are women. For example, most people see colours, when they hear.

Responsibilities of the left and right brain half

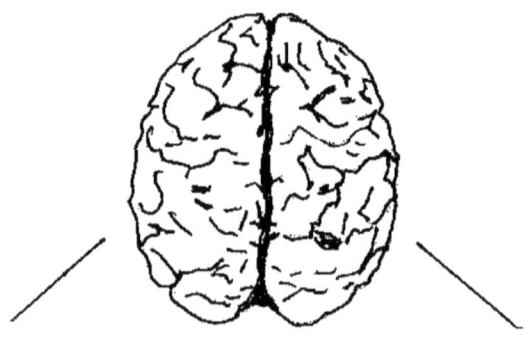

Left brain half	Right brain half
Digital information Formulas / Names / Numbers	Imagination Image capture
Rational thinking and logic	Creativity / Spontaneity
Language / Analysis	Image language / Body language
Rules / Laws	Sense of space
Thinking step by step	Feeling and intuition
Focus on one thing	Volatility
Science	Risk / Curiosity
Details	Overview / Synthesis
Coordination of the right hand	Coordination of the left hand
Sense of time	Arts / Music / Dance

When I ask you to visualize a hippopotamus as pictorially as possible, this requires a specific ability of your right brain:

> The retrieval and processing of pictorial information.

On the other hand, if I ask you to remember a number, it requires a certain ability of your left brain:

> The retrieval and processing of digital information.

But if I ask you to visualize a number as pictorially as possible, then it is in your head as in German magistrates:
Suddenly nobody feels responsible anymore!
That's also why you have trouble imagining digital information like the number above.
So, however, the question arises:

> But how do you want to remember something that you cannot even imagine?

Skat is healthy!

Have you ever thought about which brain regions in card games - such Skat - are active?
To anticipate, card games are an excellent memory training. The more demanding the game and the "opponents", the more efficient the brain jogging! So no one is surprised when an 80-year-old skat player plays a 20-year-old player into the ground. That's why Skat is - from a spiritual point of view - healthy!
Unfortunately, when playing cards, most of the regions of our left cerebral hemisphere are active, and so only these are trained, while our right brain half, so to speak, twiddles its thumps.
You certainly know that:
You make a very important business phone call that you should really focus on one hundred percent. Here, too, the brain regions of the left hemisphere * are active, for example, responsible for rational thinking, detail, analysis, rules, language, names, etc. (see page 20). So skills that are indispensable for a good card player. Nevertheless, most people do not have any difficulty in scribbling with a pen more or less beautiful little pictures or geometric shapes during the call. And yet - or even because of that - they can fully concentrate on the conversation partner.

* Hemisphere = (gr.) Earth, sky or brain half

This "picture scribbling" is inspired by the right hemisphere that is responsible for properties such as visual capture, art, music, etc. (see page 20) is responsible and that twiddles its thumps during important phone calls as well as card games.

But the abilities of the right hemisphere can be of great use, especially for remembering playing cards, numbers, names, formulas, vocabulary, and so on. The question remains, what actually speaks against, when playing cards or other thinking and memory tasks - such as the matrix tables in blackjack - to use and train your entire brain?!

In plain terms, this means that we not only give away tremendous intellectual potential, but also train our brains quite unilaterally!

> Ultimately, you only train the brain regions
> that you also use and demand!

By this self-study you will learn the techniques of memorizing, connecting, challenging and training both halves of the brain at the same time in a surprisingly simple way, so that you not only greatly improve your memory, but also your mental health promote!

For fun, try linking the left and right brain halves to a fictitious person based on their characteristics (see page 20) by constructing a personality for each hemisphere on a sheet of paper.

These keywords may include profession, gender, hobbies, passions, etc.

Brain halves and personality

What kind of profession did you associate with the fictitious person in our left hemisphere?

If you have not confused the responsibilities of the two halves of the brain, and if the left brain predicted the future of a second Renoir, you might have noted such professions as mathematicians, chemists, scientists, and so on.

Which hobbies or interests could fit the left brain half? For example, board games like Skat or Bridge, which have fixed rules that require logic, reason, analysis and concentration.

The inclinations of the left brain could also include the fact that it loves to have everything running according to fixed rules, for example, that the dinner is punctually ready at 6 o'clock or the car gets always washed on Saturday at 2 o'clock.

The fictitious person in the left half of the brain is always dressed correctly and is always on time.

What gender did you associate with the left brain? Most people will probably agree with me that these characteristics are more akin to males.

What kind of profession could the fictional person of our right brain hemisphere exercise? How about musicians or actors? But also sculptors and all other creative professions would suit it. The interests and hobbies of the right brain could include painting or dancing.

As for its inclinations, one could imagine that the fictional person of our right hemisphere sometimes comes too late to work because it simply turned around in its bed once more when the alarm rang. Even a spontaneous short trip they would hardly refuse. And what gender did you associate with the right brain?

I believe that you agree with me that we rather associate the characteristics of intuition and feeling to the female gender.

Hidden performance potential

As you can easily see, we have constructed two completely different types with our two fictional persons (brain halves). Since every human being has two halves of the brain from birth on, he also possesses their own characteristics and predispositions. Education, environment and school then decide which brain half will dominate later.

Unfortunately, both parents and schools are usually very keen to promote the characteristics and inclinations of the left brain in particular.

A fine example of this is the narrow-minded recitation of endless ballads like Goethe's "Erlkönig" or Schiller's "Song of the Bell", as we used to "experience" at school. While this was of no use, it literally made the right brain and learning motivation (the fun to learn) fall asleep with high efficiency. Consequently, one then tries later as an adult to solve the one or other task - misguided by culture and education - with the wrong brain regions. As a result, this means that we only use a part of our possible brain power and that enormous performance potential remains hidden.

> We memorize much better and faster,
> when we think in and with pictures!

Our left brain stores digital information such as names, formulas and vocabulary, etc., for example through stubborn and lengthy repetition of the information (just think of the "Erlkönig"). By nature, we find this kind of "compulsive learning" unpleasant.

The right brain, on the other hand, is capable of constructing images out of digital and thus abstract (non-objective) "things" that are not only much faster, easier and more pleasant to process for our brains, but that can also be stored much faster and easier (think of the movie with its 108,000 images in 90 minutes).

A little proof on the next page...

Names and faces of your classmates

Please try to remember all the names of your primary school classmates. You are likely to be doing pretty poorly in this test because names are digital, abstract, and processed by your left hemisphere.

Try to remember the faces of your classmates from elementary school.
You will do a lot better in this test. If your graduation is not more than 30 years ago, you will most likely be able to remember all faces because faces are pictorial information and are processed by your right hemisphere.

Although both halves of the brain, as fictitious persons, have completely different abilities and inclinations, they can work together excellently and complementarily.
If you had portrayed the "digital names" of your classmates at the time and linked these images with a peculiar characteristic of each person, you probably would still know their names today.

By illustrating digital information we connect both halves of the brain!

Structuring of the biological disk

Another common misconception when using our biological hard disk, is that you structure the "the things" you want to remember either insufficiently or not at all. Concerning this topic, I would like to tell you a little story.

*

Imagine you own a small, but well-stocked library and earn your "livelihood" by lending books. Since your longtime librarian and loyal employee went in the well-earned retirement for reasons of age, you have hired a new employee.

His job will include running the library and returning back all the books you have borrowed to their assigned place while you take care of the financial stuff.

On the first day of work of your new employee, you have a car accident on your way to your library resulting in such a complicated fractured leg that you are likely to be hospitalized for one year.

Since your new employee - according to his references - had already run a different library for many years, you do not worry about your small business, especially as you can do the business, such as bookkeeping, in the hospital bed.

At first, everything goes well. Your co-worker comes to the hospital once a week to settle accounts with you and to bring you a new book to read on each visit.

Over time, however, you realize that the revenue from your business is becoming less and less. Since you consider your new employee to be an honest person, you are initially thinking of seasonal losses.

However, after ten months of hospitalization your income is completely absent and your co-worker has not been seen for three weeks, you ask the head doctor of the hospital for early release.

You want to look after your business in your company and bring back the book you read last.

When you want to enter your library with crutches, an angry and cursing customer comes to meet you in the doorway.

When asked why he was so upset, the client just told you that he would now go to another library where you would not have to spend hours in search of the book of your choice in a mess.

When you enter your business premises, everything looks normal at first glance, so you think the customer is just a madman.

So you are going to the bookshelf with the book you last read in the hospital (a detective novel), to put it there in the space provided. Horrified, you find that there is a storybook in the place on the shelf where crime novels are usually arranged!

As you check all the other shelves, you are about to have a heart attack, as you will find that the books, sorted according to the thematic, genre, and alphabet, have been completely confused!
Now you know why the customer was so upset.
When you confront your employee, he confesses to you that his references are faked and that he initially asked customers to pick the books they wanted themselves; he would then have the books, when they were brought back, just always parked in some free space.
When you ask him why he did not put the books back in their right place, the employee replies that he cannot, he is unfortunately illiterate!

*

Presumably, it will seem perfectly logical to you that if you have several thousand books and you put them completely disordered on the shelves, they are found only with a great deal of time or with much luck again.
Therefore, you probably have your private and important documents such as purchase contracts, insurance policies, etc. also filed in appropriate folders, so they do not have to search long if necessary.
Or think about how long you would have to search on the hard disk of your computer for a document or image, if not everything was neatly sorted in folders and subfolders.

> But how do you sort and organize information,
> impressions and all other data that your brain
> is constantly confronted with?

You may well ask, you probably think now, because you know so quickly no satisfactory answer!
Thus, the ever-increasing flood of knowledge comes into our brain like into a gigantic waste bin!
Later we are surprised that if we need a specific information after days or weeks, we do not immediately find them. And we are already convinced that we have a bad memory!

Memorized playing cards, an experiment:
Part 1

Now that you have the first basic skills and knowledge to move from the brain owner to the brain user, I will literally show you how quickly you can greatly improve your memory card experience with a useful three-part experiment.

We will perform these and subsequent exercises and examples by means of a simple skat game (French playing cards). The technique, but can also be applied to all other card games and card types, such as blackjack or poker.The explanations why it works will follow later. That is why I would like to repeat my request to you again:

> Be sure to read the pages from here (after the coffee cup) to page 55 in one piece!

The time required for this, including the breaks and exercises, is about two hours.

Make yourself comfortable in your own personal learning environment and make sure that you do not get disturbed or interrupted.

If you have this time now, please have a writing pad and pen ready, and let us start the experiment.

Test with 30 playing cards

First, we will use a small memory exercise to determine the current state of your card memory. Please, try to relax and eliminate any factors that may distract you from this exercise in any way, such as a TV running in the background or a radio-roaring in the kitchen, so that you can fully concentrate on your exercise.

Below is a list of 30 playing cards. Your task is to memorize as many of the cards in their order as possible by reading this list once, slowly.

*

1. = Ten of spades (10)	16. = Eight of clubs (8)
2. = Queen of diamonds	17. = Ace of clubs
3. = Nine of hearts (9)	18. = Ace of spades
4. = Jack of hearts	19. = Jack of spades
5. = Seven of spades (7)	20. = Queen of hearts
6. = King of spades	21. = Eight of spades (8)
7. = Jack of clubs	22. = Eight of diamonds (8)
8. = Nine of spades (9)	23. = King of hearts
9. = Ten of clubs (10)	24. = Seven of diamonds (7)
10. = King of diamonds	25. = Ace of hearts
11. = Ten of diamonds (10)	26. = Jack of diamonds
12. = Queen of clubs	27. = Queen of spades
13. = Seven of hearts (7)	28. = Ten of hearts (10)
14. = King of clubs	29. = Seven of clubs (7)
15. = Eight of hearts (8)	30. = Nine of diamonds (9)

You will probably shake your head or tear your hair, when seeing the list according to the motto:

"I cannot do that anyway."

Or: "How is this supposed to work?"

Nevertheless, try it once! This exercise is only for the purpose of determining your current ability to memorize playing cards. Based on the result, you can later assess the improvement in your memory performance.

Even though your head might be smoking right now, I would like to ask you to number a sheet of paper on the left side from 1 to 30.

Now try to assign as many playing cards as possible to your position from your memory. Take as much time as you like and try to really play the cards out of your memory.

As mentioned earlier, this exercise is not about breaking any records (try that later), but about determining the current state of your card memory.

Please compare your list with the list on page 29!

Look forward to something completely new!

And, how did you perform? You think, you did not so well? If you have correctly remembered about 3 to 6 cards, that is perfectly normal, and about 95% of your fellow human beings will do just about the same in this test.

If you have been able to remember more than 6 or even up to 10 cards, you are already an exception, or you have already worked with your own technique. If you were able to write down all 30 playing cards in the correct order, I would like to congratulate you. Surely there is a nice person in your circle of friends who appreciates this book as a gift.

Honestly, how did you feel emotionally about this first exercise? Was it rather exhausting and stressful? Or has this exercise even caused you unpleasant associations?

For example, emotional connections that may have reminded you of your school time, when you had to memorize some poems, such as the "Erlkönig" or "The Song of the Bell", and then, despite weeks of agony, got a bad grade, just because you got stuck at one line?

Under these circumstances, it would even be conceivable that the learning frustration learned from your earliest childhood triggered some kind of learning blockade in your subconscious mind.

I can prove to you with the following experiment that learning is also fun and at the same time - due to the resulting learning motivation - can be many times more efficient.

For our experiment to be successful,
I would like to ask you two things:

1. Do whatever I ask you to do, even - and this is very important - if some things seem crazy or even strange to you. Concerning the meaning of this or that action or activity I will deliberately not yet enter into this point, because I want you to focus initially on the practice only. After all, it is the practical things that convince us!

Let us pick up the theory, the logic and the science for a later time, and you will see, it works that way!

2. Also, I would like to ask you to try and get your mind free for our experiment, as if you were a child again. After all, children have the ingenious ability to be completely unprejudiced with completely new things.

In contrast to us adults, we often have stuck opinions and prejudices. Just be curious about something you have not known before.

During this self-learning course forget for once everything you have been taught about learning techniques. Even if you should be a teacher.

Let us do a blind eye for our experiment.

Instead, look forward to trying something completely new, just as you enjoyed constantly discovering something new as a child! If you believe to meet both requirements, you are well prepared to begin our experiment.

Memorized playing cards, an experiment: Part 2

Let us start our experiment with a small gymnastic insert.
As I said, do not be surprised, just do what I ask you to do!
One more note: If, for health reasons, you are unable to practice the exercises below, improvise by at least mentally copying them.
Please, however, do not give up by any means only as a matter of convenience!

*

If you are sitting, I would like to ask you to get up and drop your book, so you can easily read the following lines.

1. Now stretch your arms forward and do a forward bend to touch the shoes with your fingertips. Say aloud: "Shoes: Position 1". Please note: your shoes are the 1st position.

2. Now set yourself up again and adopt your attitude. Of course, I do not mean that you sit down again, but that you stand upright! Next, use your palms to touch both kneecaps and say aloud, "Position 2".
Your kneecaps are now position 2 on your "body list."
Please memorize these and the following eight positions well.

3. Go back to your starting position, touch your thighs and say aloud: "Position 3".

4. Now, touch your buttocks with both palms of your hands as you announce: this is your "Position 4".

5. Now, put both arms and hands on your hips, just as if you were trying to scold someone, and say aloud, "Position 5".

6. Now put your hands on your chest as if you were terribly frightened and shout: "Position 6".

7. Next, place your right hand on the left shoulder and your left hand on your right shoulder and say aloud: "Position 7".

8. Now, hold your neck with all ten fingers and say aloud: "Position 8".

9. Touch your nose with both hands. Your nose is "Position 9".

10. Perhaps you would like to tear your hair at the apparent nonsense I asked you to do? All right, but not without loudly saying "Position 10".
Your hair is the tenth and last position on your body list.

Since it is of great importance that you master your body list almost as if you were asleep, I recommend that you repeat this exercise a few more times - even in the reverse order.

This was the second and at the same time physically demanding part of our experiment. As mentioned before, it is very important that you master the order of your body positions perfectly.
For example, if I call the number "5," you should know immediately that this is your hip. In the beginning, you might still have some difficulties. This is completely normal and is partly due to the fact that the exercise seems a bit strange to you, and secondly, that you are simply still inexperienced.

As crazy as possible

For the third and final part of our experiment, it is of the utmost importance that you visualize the following images and stories as fluid, dramatic, peppy and colourful as possible in your imagination.

This also means that you decorate your fantasy images with all your senses and sensations. These include: smelling, tasting, hearing and feeling, especially feelings of happiness, pain, hate, eroticism, shame, and anything else you can feel.

Make pictures in your imagination that are as crazy as possible, which I cannot actually occur in reality. The more unusual and unlikely your pictures are, the better you will be able to remember these pictures, because these pictures IMPRESS you in the truest sense of the word!

Memorized playing cards, an experiment: Part 3

I want you to look at your right shoe or, if you do not wear a shoe, just look at your foot, which represents the first of ten positions on your body list.

Imagine as figurative as possible, over your foot drives a huge bulldozer! Imagine driving over your foot with rattling drive chains and deafening diesel engine noise. Try to imagine this picture as intense as possible. Feel the pain caused by the great weight of the bulldozer on your foot. Do you smell the stinking diesel exhaust? What kind of shape and color does the bulldozer have?

Is it perhaps shaped like a cast-iron rectangle with curb chains that has a huge, rusty shovel in front, and painted yellow except for the mud-smeared drive chains and scattered everywhere with small and larger rust stains?

Construct as many details and sensations as possible! Especially, bring in movement. Bring yourself or other people who are familiar or unfamiliar to you, such as actors, fairy tale characters, politicians and athletes, but also animals into these moving images.

Castle damsel with a bulldozer

As you take a closer look at the bulldozer on your foot, you can see who is operating the levers on the cab.

It is a castle damsel, who seems to have come from the Middle Ages. A delicate female, as you only know it only from knight films, with the typical, about half a meter high pointed hat. Just a damsel of the castle, who attaches the knight her silky handkerchief to the knight after the won tournament. Her immaculate blue silk dress and the delicate tulle in front of her face are nowhere near the dirty and crude bulldozer.

And what is the castle damsel pushing with the rusty shovel of her bulldozer? Incredible, a huge pile of thousands of bridal bouquets resembling the little Biedermeier bouquets with paper bristles. And how well the bridal bouquets smell! They smell so intense that they almost cover the diesel smell of the bulldozer.

I hope you enjoyed this little foot story, and I'm sure if I ask you what has just crossed your foot, you will immediately come across the bulldozer!

If we summarize this little foot story in three words, we have:

1st = Bulldozer - 2nd = Castle damsel - 3rd = Bridal bouquets

Very important!

I would like to ask you to repeat this and the following nine stories in your mind with your imagination for a minute or two, in your mind's eye, so to speak.

An incredibly fat baby

Next, I will present you with a little knee story, in which you please imagine as much as possible.

An incredibly fat baby sits on your right knee. A baby that weighs at least 30 pounds and is more reminiscent of a Michelin Man. This baby is wearing only a diaper and screams terribly. From lots of crying, the child's head has already got the signal colour of a fire alarm. Of course, you're wondering why the baby is screaming so terribly, and you are already worried that your knee might be wetted with a moist, rather than fragrant liquid at any second.

Suddenly, the baby quickly brings out his left hand behind his back, where it holds the miniature version of a small earth hoe. An earth hoe, as commonly used in field work or in the garden.

This skin of the "Michelin Man" turns on the head and leaves his left hand - including the earth hoe - quickly disappear behind his back.

Now it becomes clear to you why the giant baby screams so terribly and has such a red head: because it always strikes itself again and again with his earth hoe on the head!

Since you are sorry and you are a good person, drive your car to the next hardware store and buy a construction helmet for the child.

Once at home, take the screaming giant baby back on your right knee and put the helmet on the child's head. Exactly a second later, the baby's left hand jumps out again with the earth hoe and hits the helmet with a loud clacking sound.

Now since the child did not feel any pain, it suddenly stops screaming, and the red color disappears from its face!

Now, looking at your knee - your position 2 - you automatically remember our little knee story, which is summarized in three words:

1st = Baby - 2nd = Earth hoe - 3rd = Helmet

Please, also remember this little story again mentally, and then return to the book.

A transformation

Imagine, it is just before Christmas, and you have inexpensive purchased a nativity scene at the Christmas market. Since you were in a hurry, you have not seen or tested the contents of the packaging. Now you sit in your living room comfortably at the fireplace and have the already unpacked nativity scene on your thighs (third position of your body list) asked to look at your new acquisition more closely.

As you look inside the crib, you do not believe your eyes! There, where there is usually the nativity scene with the baby Jesus for a bed, there is an ordinary wheelbarrow. An old, rusty wheelbarrow whose only rubber tire in the front has a flat tire.

But now you want to know more about it, and use your pointed fingers to slowly and carefully pull the wheelbarrow out of the crib to check out what is probably in the back of the truck bed.

Just when you bring out the old and rusty wheelbarrow, it turns into a bible! And not in any bible, but in a glorious, gold-framed, pearl-studded and precious-stone bible of inestimable value!

You touch your thighs (position 3) and immediately know how our thigh story is summed up in three words:

1st = Nativity scene - 2nd = Wheelbarrow - 3rd = Bible

Please repeat this story again on your mind.

A wonderful day?

Please imagine the following situation: It is a beautiful day, and you decide to use the beautiful weather for a walk. While you leisurely stroll along the sidewalk, enjoying the fresh air and the warm sunshine, listen to the song of an obviously cheerful bird. Suddenly the bird stops singing. Instead, you hear a sound from behind that increases rapidly and intensively in volume. The next second, you realize that these are the hoofbeats of a galloping horse. Amazed, you stop to look over your shoulder. Now you see a knight riding in shiny armor.

You panic and almost freeze in horror as you realize that he is holding a lance in his right hand with which he is obviously aiming at their rear. And indeed, as soon as you have thought through your apprehension, you feel a terribly piercing pain on your butt, and the Knight's lance has struck its target with fateful precision!

At the same time the horse stumbles, the knight falls headlong on the sidewalk with loud clanking armor, breaks his neck and dies at his own crime scene. Your butt hurts that hard now, so that you become unconscious. When you awake again, a black-clad woman stands in front of you, insulting you and accusing you of being a widow because of you.

You had a pretty dramatic walk, do not you think so?
It is also quite unfair what the widow of the knight accuses you of.
After all, it was the knight's fault that he bent his tin cap.

And anyway, what is your butt doing? By what did you get hurt again there?
Oh yes, right! By a spear, so you will instantly remember our story summarized in three words, if you think of your butt (position 4).

1st = Knight - 2nd = Lance - 3rd = Widow

Try to experience this afternoon again in your mind's eye.

A great birthday present

Here is a description that I have come up with for the fifth position of the body list, your hip.
Imagine, you have your birthday and get a great belt from a friend. This belt was designed by a Russian artist and is a real unique one.
The belt buckle consists of a palm-sized, enamelled, bright green cloverleaf, which somehow feels strange and cool.
On the leather of the belt there are tiny Russian icons attached!

At each icon there is a small eyelet at the bottom attached to a chain, consisting of five golden wedding rings. As you put the belt around your waist, these wedding ring chains jingle quite oddly.
The fifth story, summarized in three words, is:

1st = Cloverleaf - 2nd = Icon - 3rd = Wedding ring

Please internalize again the description of your birthday present, and then return here again.

Five times MEMORABLE in a nutshel

With the recent story and the associated fifth position, you have been able to mentally experience half of a total of ten small and memorable stories that I came up with for our experiment with the body list.

Before we come to the sixth story, I would like to summarize with you the previous - because of their deeper meaning - again in a nutshell. Do not be surprised, just remember:

> **Exceptional performance require**
> **extraordinary activities!**

What three things do you see in your mind's eye when you look at your foot - the 1st position on your body list?

You probably will not have any trouble remembering the bulldozer, which rattled painfully over your foot with its rattling chains and stinking diesel exhaust fumes.

And who steered the bulldozer?

The delicate castle damsel, who had just emerged from the Middle Ages and with her pointed hat and the blue silk dress which did not fit into this rough bulldozer.

What was the damsel pushing with the rusty shovel of her bulldozer?

Correct! A huge pile of bridal bouquets. And the flowers smelled so good that their smell almost covered the foul diesel exhaust of the bulldozer.

> The keywords in your position 1 (your foot) are:
>
> **1st = Bulldozer - 2nd = Castle damsel - 3rd = Bridal bouquets**

Who or what was actually sitting on your position 2, the knee?

I agree! An incredibly fat baby that weighed at least 30 pounds and was more reminiscent of the Michelin Man than a baby.

Surely, you also know that this baby screamed terribly, so that the head of the baby was already completely red and you had to fear for your pants.

Very quickly, however, you had found out the true reason for the crying of the baby. It had always hit itself on the head with an object! Do you still remember which item it was?

Correct! An earth hoe, more precisely, the miniature version of an earth hoe, as commonly used in field work or in the garden.

And what did you do to help the baby?
Naturally! You had put a helmet on the child's head, so that there is only a loud clacking sound when the baby hits his head with his earth hoe.

The keywords on your position 2 (your knee) are:

1st = Baby - 2nd = Earth hoe - 3rd = Helmet

What do you think or what do you see when you look at your thighs (position 3)?

I agree! A nativity scene, but a nativity scene that literally has it!
Where else is the manger that has been misappropriated for our baby Jesus?
Again right! A wheelbarrow, a nasty old and rusty wheelbarrow. When you pulled the wheelbarrow out of the nativity scene with your pointed fingers to check what was in the back of the truck, did the wheelbarrow turn into something?
Correct! Into a bible, not into any bible, but into a glorious Bible set in pure gold, filled with pearls and gems, invaluable.

The keywords on your position 3 (your thigh):

1st = Nativity scene – 2nd = Wheelbarrow – 3nd = Bible

What comes to your mind spontaneously when I ask you now whether you can sit down again without any problems and especially all without pain?

It probably reminds you of the dramatic story that took place in your position 4, the butt.
Who was responsible for the whole dilemma?
Of course, the knight! That knight in his shining armor who had attacked you from behind during your walk from his galloping horse and for no reason at all.
Surely, you will also remember painfully with what the knight had stabbed you so accurate in the butt?
Exactly! With his lance!
And what happened to the knight after he stabbed?
His horse stumbled, and the knight fell headlong on the sidewalk, clawing his armor, breaking his neck and dying. Your pain became so severe that you became unconscious. When you awoke again, you saw the widow of

at the knight, dressed in black telling you that she is a widow because of you.

Try describing the belt you were given for your birthday and strapping it around your hips (position 5). Do you remember what the belt buckle looked like?

Right, like a cloverleaf! A palm-sized, bright green, enameled shamrock that felt oddly cool and smooth. This great belt was designed by a Russian artist who had put something on the whole length of the belt.
Right, tiny icons, each with a small eyelet attached to its lower edge. Do you also know what was hanging on these eyelets?
Exactly, wedding rings, each assembled in a chain of five, jingling in a strange way as you strapped on your birthday present.

I would now like to ask you to review these little stories again in your mind's eye. Try to imagine these stories with all your senses, such as smelling, tasting, feeling and hearing, in your imagination. Make these pictures as crazy, shrill, loud and colorful as you can. Exaggerate excessively, incorporate feelings such as pleasure, joy, fun in your pictures, but also anger, argument and frustration.

These pictures must be as moving as possible. Build yourself into these stories to make your pictures even more intense. The clearer you have them in your mind, the better you will remember them. Then treat yourself a little break and return back here.

Like vultures

Welcome to the last five stories of the experiment.

Imagine being lying on your back with your eyes closed. Suddenly you feel an increasing pressure on your chest (position 6), as if someone had put something incredibly heavy on your chest. And indeed, when you open your eyes, there is a massive tombstone on your chest!

On this tombstone, however, there is not as expected a name, but engraved in golden letters: "He had more redwine than sunshine."

While you enjoy this funny saying, a vulture lands on the top of the tombstone.

The vulture has something long and sharp in its right claw. As you look more closely, and especially astude, you realize that the tool is a branch saw.

The friendly vulture throws you the branch saw and tells you to saw off the tombstone on your chest at the bottom.

You follow its request, and the vulture flies away with the tombstone.

By the way, if you ask me for the title of this little story, I can only shrug my shoulders and say:

"Like vultures – God only knows!"

The story on position 6 (of your chest) summarized in three words reads:

1st = Tombstone - 2nd = Vulture - 3rd = Branch saw

Please, repeat this story with all your phantasy again.

A sandy matter

For the 7th position of your body list - your shoulders - I have come up with a pretty sandy story. Imagine, you are looking at your left shoulder because you think you heard a strange noise from there.
And indeed, on your shoulder you can see a small sandbox, as well as children use to play in. In this sandbox, however, there are no children playing, but there is a completely white dressed woman. As you look closer, you see that the woman is not just wearing a plain white dress, but that the dress is a sumptuous wedding dress.

Obviously, the bride wants to laboriously shovel all the sand out of the sandpit. But the bride does not shovel, as one might think, with a shovel, but with a huge concrete pipe, a concrete pipe normally used for sewer construction.

Again summarized in three words, you saw on your shoulder:

1st = Sandbox - 2nd = Bride - 3rd = Concrete pipe

Before you continue with the eighth story, please try to bring the scene on your shoulder to mind once more.

A journey to the Middle Ages

For our eighth story - your neck position - we take a little trip to the Middle Ages. Imagine being in your bed and having a dream. You dream you are in the courtyard of a medieval castle. There you see a pitiable man who has to carry a yoke around his neck because he stole an apple from the lord of the castle. This excessive and exaggerated punishment will make you so excited that you wake up.

As you slowly realize that it was all just a dream, you are horrified to find that you are now wearing this yoke around your neck! Panicked, you jump out of bed and want to leave your bedroom to take a closer look in the bathroom mirror.

When you open your bedroom door, a newlywed bridal couple is standing in front of you. You are astonished to see the groom raise his right hand holding a heavy medieval battle ax. Before you can react, the groom hits your neck-mounted yoke with his battle ax.
Right, now you are really awake!

1st = Yoke - 2nd = Bridegroom - 3rd = Battle ax

Even after this story, please take another two or three minutes to let your imagination run free.

Fanfare as a coachman whip

Surely you are looking forward to our ninth and penultimate story that will take place on your nose - the position 9 - and begins as follows:

Something crawls around on your nose bone. At first, you suspect that an insect has settled on your nose. However, when you squint with both eyes towards your nose, you see a snow-white wedding carriage pulled by six white horses.

On the coach sits a small, fat squire, who remembers the squires of Don Quixote with his funny and colorful costume.

With a fanfare - as a substitute for a coachman's whip - he meets the poor horses like crazy, so that the wedding car moves again and again with rapid speed up and down.

Suddenly the wedding carriage stops, a woman stands up and gets out. As you look closer, you realize that this woman is Alice Schwarzer.* Alice Schwarzer scolds terribly with the squire and takes away his "whip".

The ninth story you have experienced on your nose can be summarized in three words:

1st = Wedding carriage - 2nd = Squire - 3rd = Alice Schwarzer

Please also review this story in your mind. Then come back to our last story here.

* Alice Schwarzer = well-known German women's rights activist

Ripping your hair?

Let us now turn to our tenth and last story, which of course is related to the 10th position of your body list - the hair!
Please put yourself in the following situation:
You enter a hat shop to buy a new hat. A hat catches your eye, even though it is in the far corner of the shop.
Immediately, you try on the hat to look at it in the mirror. When you look in the mirror, you feel like you cannot trust your eyes.
What you suddenly see on your head is not a hat, but a miniature bed. And you already notice how the four legs of the bed cause uncomfortable pressure points on your scalp due to the weight.
Strangely, a glass coffin lies on the bed instead of a blanket, as we all know it from the fairy tale "Snow White and the seven Dwarfs".

Suddenly, with a loud creaking sound, the casket lid opens, and a small, but rather lively little man with a big flag jumps out.
There is only one word on this flag: END.

That was literally a story for "ripping your hair"! The little man has indicated with his flag the end of the tenth and last history of our experiment. However, this does not mean that we are finished with our self-study.

Our tenth and final story, summarized in three words, is:

1st = Bed - 2nd = Coffin - 3rd = Flag

Please experience the story "Ripping your hair" again in your imagination and then return to the book!

MEMORABLE - Summarized from six to ten

Like the stories from 1 to 5, we will summarize those from 6 to 10 again. We start with the 6th position of your body list, the chest.

Do you remember what you saw when you laid on your back and opened your eyes, because you felt so much pressure on your chest?
Exactly, a tombstone!
A tombstone with a funny saying, which read:
"He had more redwine than sunshine".

What landed on the top of the tombstone?
Right again! A vulture!
This friendly vulture wanted to help you out of your predicament and had something in his claw for that purpose - especially for you.
What tool was that? Of course, the saw!
A branch saw with which you sawed off the tombstone on your chest so that the vulture could fly away with it.

The keywords on your position 6 (your chest) are:

1st = Tombstone - 2nd = Vulture - 3rd = Branch saw

It continues with the 7th position of your body list, the shoulders. Can you still remember what you saw on your left shoulder? Right, a sandbox!

And who set about emptying the sandbox in laborious hard work?
Of course, the bride!
A bride in a gorgeous white bridal gown.

Surely, you also know that the bride did not do this job, as one would expect, with a shovel, but with what?
Exactly, with a concrete pipe!
A concrete pipe normally used for sewer construction.

> The keywords on your position 7 (your shoulder) are:
>
> **1st = Sandbox - 2nd = Bride - 3rd = Concrete pipe**

Now try to remember which story you associate with your position 8, the neck.
Think of your little trip to the Middle Ages.

If you hold your hand around your neck, you are relieved that there is no yoke there!

It probably would not be very likely that in front of your bedroom door a newlywed bride and groom and the groom strikes with a medieval battle ax on your yoke.

Nevertheless, you know:

> The keywords in your position 8 (your neck) are:
>
> **1st = Yoke - 2nd = Bridegroom - 3rd = Battle ax**

Do you remember who or what literally "always followed your nose"?
Correct! The snow-white wedding carriage pulled by six white horses.

And who drove the carriage up and down on your nose at breakneck speed?

I agree! A squire, with his funny and colorful costume reminded of the squires of Don Quixote and had beaten repeatedly from his coachman with his fanfare as a whip replacement on the poor horses.

Surely you also know who the passenger in this wedding carriage was? Right again! Alice Schwarzer, who scolded the squire terribly and took his "whip" from him.

> The keywords on your position 9 (of your nose) are:
>
> **1st = Wedding carriage - 2nd = Squire - 3rd = Alice Schwarzer**

Even our tenth and last story, which was really "ripping your hair", should not be too difficult to remember!
When you looked in the mirror in the hat shop, you saw something on your head?
Correct! A bed that has left uncomfortable pressure points on your scalp with its four legs.

And what was lying on the bed instead of a blanket?
Right again! A coffin, a glass coffin, as you know it, for example, from the fairy tale Snow White and the Seven Dwarfs.

Suddenly the coffin lid was opened with a loud creaking sound, and a merry little man jumped out. Do you remember what the little man waved so excitedly?
Exactly, a flag! A banner with the inscription: END.

> The keywords on your position 10 (your hair) are:
>
> **1st = Bed - 2nd = Coffin - 3rd = Flag**

All keywords
- on the body list -
in the overview

Position 1	Foot	1st = Bulldozer 2nd = Castle damsel 3rd = Bridal bouquet
Position 2	Knee	1st = Baby 2nd = Earth hoe 3rd = Helmet
Position 3	Thigh	1st = Natavity scene 2nd = Wheelbarrow 3rd = Bible
Position 4	Buttocks	1st = Knight 2nd = Lance 3rd = Widow
Position 5	Hip	1st = Cloverleaf 2nd = Icon 3rd = Wedding ring
Position 6	Chest	1st = Tombstone 2nd = Vulture 3rd = Astute saw
Position 7	Shoulder	1st = Sandbox 2nd = Bride 3rd = Concrete pipe
Position 8	Neck	1st = Yoke 2nd = Groom 3rd = Battle axe
Position 9	Nose	1st = Wedding carriage 2nd = Squire 3rd = Alice Schwarzer
Position 10	Hair	1st = Bed 2nd = Coffin 3rd = Flag

Compare once

I would like to ask you to pick up your pad again and number it on the left side from one to ten.

Then, from your memory, try repeating the 10 positions of your body list in the correct order, for example:

Position 1 is Foot.
Position 2 is ....?

Then compare your result with the keywords overview (see above). How many of the ten positions on your body list did you list in the right order?
If you were not distracted or interrupted during the experiment, you will most likely have solved this problem 100%.

Somewhat more difficult should already be your next task.
Now, please, try to assign the corresponding three keywords in the right order to the individual positions of your body list.

For example:
Position 1 is Foot.
Key words are:
1st = Bulldozer, 2nd = Castle damsel, 3rd = Bridal bouquet.

Position 2 is Knee.
Keywords are:
1st = ...? 2nd = ...? 3rd = ...?

Important!
Take a lot of time for this task and try to remember as many details of the stories as possible. Then compare your result again with the keywords - overview on page 54.
I wish you much success.

First AHA - experiences

You probably had no trouble remembering 20 or more keywords! If you did our experiment with full concentration and calmness, it would not even be unusual if you could even remember all the positions, including their keywords, in the right order.

If you remember fewer than 15 key words or even can not name the individual positions on your body list in the correct order, then that is not a big deal. Maybe you were just interrupted by some disturbing influences, such as the constant telephone ringing or something similar, again and again during your self-study. Nevertheless, in this case, I recommend that you start over from scratch with our experiment. For learning the technique it is of utmost importance that the exercises are performed exactly as described.

Please remember our first exercise when you tried to remember 30 playing cards in order to determine the now-state of your card memory.

Compare the list of playing cards you could reproduce from your memory with the list of your 10 body positions and the 30 keyframes you could write down.

For both lists, you tried to remember as many objects as possible in their order. Which of the two lists did you find simpler? Or vice versa, how many corrects did you have in the list of the 30 playing cards, and how many of the 10 positions of your body list or 30 keyframes could you remember?

Without looking at your list, can you tell me which one was the 6th card on your playing card list? Hardly likely!

But if I ask you which key frame on your body list is number 6, you will probably only think for a moment and know that this is the 3rd key frame on the 2nd position of your body list – the knee - and you can answer "Helmet".

As a result, you cannot only remember the second list much better, but you can even say exactly where, with what number, what is! You could not do the same thing with the playing card list even if you memorized their order, because you always have to count the cards in your mind.

The deeper meaning

At first I mentioned that the little and strange stories make a deeper sense.

> It is particularly brain-friendly, when we think in pictures!
> The technical term for this is:
> Elemental association

All 10 positions of your body list are covered with three keyframes. So on your body list there are 30 keyframes in a specific order!
Each of these thirty keyframes corresponds to one of the thirty playing cards on the playing card list (page 29) in exactly this order.

Before you read on, I would like to ask you to have a brief look at the keyframe list on pages 140 to 142.

What is meant by substitute pictures and subject areas or how does the technique of the card feature work as a whole, I will explain this later. For me it was very important that you first have a practical sense of achievement.
Before turning back to the playing cards, I will explain to you, using other, simpler, but still very useful hinting techniques why you could remember the keyframes on your body list much better than the playing card list.

Remembering names made easy

On page 25, I asked you to try again to remember all the names of your classmates from primary school.

Since names - like playing cards - are digital and thus abstract information, they are processed by your left brain. You probably had a pretty bad result in this test.

I also asked you to remember the faces (pictorial information) of your classmates for whom your right hemisphere is responsible. Surely, you have done far better in this test because faces are pictorial information and, as you have noticed, images are especially memorable for our brains! That is the reason why it is said that:

A picture is worth a thousand words!

Two small examples:

➢ Try to use words to describe the hippopotamus on page 19 that you had in your mind's eye in a matter of seconds.

➢ Or think again of the feature film on page 15 with its 108,000 images in 90 minutes.

So, you SEE, even though both halves of the brain – if you imagine them as fictional people – have completely different abilities and inclinations, they can work together well and complement each other.

On page 25, I said that if you had portrayed the (digital) names of your classmates back then, and linked those images to a specific attribute of each person, you probably would still know them today. I would like to give you a short example. It is also important here that you decorate the images as imaginative as possible.

The technique

Imagine being invited to a party and being introduced to someone. Let us say this person is a man and his German name is Wolfgang Berghammer. While you shake hands with Mr. Berghammer and introduce yourself, you seek a reference point for your new acquaintance. If possible, this reference point should immediately catch your eye, so be as distinctive as possible.

It could be a particularly tasteful or tasteless garment or piece of jewelry, the glasses, the hairstyle or even physical features. The only important thing is that it is a noticeable detail that you can associate with this person!

For example, let us imagine that Mr. Wolfgang Berghammer has a strikingly polished bald head, shaped like the "pointed" side of a hen's egg. You have now found your distinctive point that you can associate with this person and their name.

Next, associate the reference point with the name by merging both into one image.
The surname Berghammer is composed of the German words "Berg" and "Hammer".
The German word >Berg< is "Mountain" in English.
The German word >Hammer< is also "Hammer" in English.
For this you could imagine that this bald is a mountain on which a huge hammer instead of a summit cross is located.
The "bald" - I mean, your new acquaintance - is called by last name:
BERG-HAMMER.

The first name Wolfgang is composed of the German words "Wolf" and "Gang".
The German word >Wolf< is "Wolf" in English.
The German word >Gang< is "Walking" in English.
WOLF-GANG

Now imagine that a wolf is constantly going around this mountain, and every time it has completed a new round and comes into view, the wolf raises its leg; and the hammer disappears loudly with its stem thunderous in the mountain.
If, after an hour, this person meets you again at the party, you know immediately that the "bald" is Wolfgang Berghammer.

> However, the condition is that you really have these pictures crystal clear and alive in your mind's eye.

If you repeat these connections in the next three to six days in total six to eight times mentally, you also know in half a year that the man with the bald head is Wolfgang Berghammer!
Try to memorize as many names as possible at an event this way. Or take an illustrated newspaper to practice with pictures of people named by name you do not know yet. You will find that you develop an excellent memory.

For one or the other, these fantasy images and stories are quite difficult at first. The fact is, the more difficulties you have, the more "half-brained" you have used your mental potential or the more your dominant left brain has suppressed or superimposed the capabilities of your right hemisphere.

Therefore, especially those who have great difficulties should be very motivated to practice, because previously untapped brain potential has finally been released for use. Remember you train and challenge only the brain regions that you use.

> Just a little practice, and you will be amazed how fast
> you can exploit these potentials for yourself
> and benefit from your entire brain in the future, as well!

But if you are firmly convinced that you cannot "produce" images in your mind, then I ask you:

How do you actually dream? In words?!

So much - at first – about imagening digital information.

Remembering by location

This chapter is about structuring the biological hard disk (see page 26). Surely, your new, more specifically, former employee, who in truth was an illiterate and randomly sorted the books into the shelves of the library, will come to your mind.

Or your computer or how long you would have to search on the hard drive for a document or image if everything was not neatly sorted into folders and subfolders.

I would also like to address this very important topic with a practical example.

Crib sheet in the head

In the meantime, it seems logical to put new information and data that is important to you in your memory. A first example of this was the body list (from foot to hair), by which you could save the keyframes (playing card images) in the correct order.

Furthermore, you took advantage of the bald spot of Mr. Wolfgang Berghammer as a reference point and folder.

I would like to show you the tremendous benefits that this knowledge can bring you in completely different everyday situations, e.g. using a shopping list.

Imagine that you have no paper or pen and you have to remember the following shopping list with the ten different products in their order.

Your crib sheet – Shopping list

1.	Fish
2.	Bread
3.	Mustard
4.	Shampoo
5.	Beef
6.	Cheese spread
7.	Tights
8.	Headache pills
9.	Spaghetti sauce
10.	Eggs

In future you can benefit from your simple, but very useful body list concerning such situations, as well!

Please link - after the next pause sign - the ten products of the shopping list with the ten positions of your body list. By linking, I mean that you introduce yourself to the products of your grocery list as crazy and moving images again and assign them to the positions of your body list. Proceed in the same way as in our experiment with the key or card images.

Here is an example:
The first product on your shopping list is fish. You could imagine, there would fidget a two-meter-long silvery-shiny fish on your shoes (foot is position 1 of your body list). And it does not only stink terribly, but also pollutes your freshly cleaned shoes by its slimy and glibly scales skin.

Try this little experiment once in a hurry, and gradually add the ten products from the shopping list to your body list.

Let your imagination run free, and produce your pictures as clearly as possible, as with the keyframes in our first experiment.

Take a lot of time and do not put yourself under pressure. This is not about the speed with which you prove the list, but about something I can tell you later for "tactical" reasons.

If you think you can enumerate your grocery list in the correct order, take a ten-minute break and then try to reconstruct the list from your memory.

If you look once again at your crib sheet or shopping list, you probably will not have any difficulty remembering which products are in which position. You will be able to easily reproduce this shopping list from your memory, because you did not remember the names of the products, but changed the names into pictures and arranged them additionally - with the help of the body list.
That means:

> If we want to remember digital information quickly and safely, you have to turn them into pictures and sort them out in a Brain-friendly way!
> - Remember the hippopotamus and the librarian -

If you have children

If you have children or grandchildren of pre-school age, try to teach them the body list in a playful way.
Next, try working with the child to put your latest shopping list on the child's body list in the form of funny little stories.
Take the child to your next purchase and pretend to have forgotten your shopping list again. If you then leave the "directing" and the order of purchase to the child and allow yourself to be guided to the required products, you will wonder what tremendous learning motivation a child can develop even with such a "dry learning material" as a shopping list!

> And your child will remember:
> Learning does not necessarily hurt!

The ancient Greeks

The procedure just described is called elemental association, and it has its origins in ancient Greek mnemonics. The term mnemonics is derived from the Greek word "mnemoniká," which means "memory." Namesake is the goddess of memory Mnemosyne, which is also known as the mother of all muses.
This technique is not only extremely user-friendly for our memory of tremendous efficiency, but also for our entire brain, because both halves of the brain are simultaneously synchronized with this method!

But not only the ancient Greeks, but also the Romans have developed and applied such lists with the so-called loci method (locus = the place) for the purpose of better memory. Better known is the Roman memory technique called "temple list".

As you can certainly imagine, this technique is not the very latest.

More specifically, they have been around for more than 2,500 years. This knowledge used to be available only to scholars and privileged people. With the invention of printing, the knowledge of these techniques was almost completely lost, because one believed that one did not have to "keep much in mind", since one had to only look it up in the book, if one really forgot something.

So much in a nutshell to the historical roots of these techniques.

Also, the technique for remembering playing cards is based on the two aforementioned techniques and works similarly in principle.

Some extras and additions

As an example, take the seventh product (tights) on our shopping list, which you have combined with the 7th position of your body list (shoulder) to form a holistic picture. When you tried to construct a picture for your shoulder in your head, it might have been relatively easy for you, because you had your shoulder as a picture "in the true sense of the word" in mind.

For the image of the tights you should have already done a bit more brain work. For this you literally had to "straighten out" a picture, as I had not clearly defined on the shopping list what material these tights consist of. For example, it could be a silk, wool or nylon tights.

Furthermore, you had to be aware of the color, shape or texture of the tights in order to get a clear picture of the product. So you had to produce the image of the tights with all their details in your head!

Also for the playing card technology we have to map the card values, only you have it much easier. At first, you only need to visualize your card images once and not "reprint" any pictures anew each time.

Perhaps you will object now: "If I have a playing card, then that is a picture!" Unfortunately not, for example, a playing card is perceived or processed as a digital value of your left hemisphere while playing cards, not as a picture.

However, if you are still convinced that a playing card is a picture for our brains, I would suggest the following experiment:

Mix a card game with 30 cards. Then I want you to proceed with the individual cards as well as in our experiment with the keyframes. So you begin again with your foot as position 1, there by the thoughtful succession drop the first three cards and come up with a story. That could sound like this:

On my foot is a ten of spades, suddenly a queen of diamonds comes from the right, and because the queen of diamonds has now come from the right, the nine of hearts comes from the left. Do the whole thing with all 30 playing cards on your ten positions of the body list and then return to the book.

And how did it succeed? Did you notice how difficult it is to imagine a story with the digital information of the playing cards?

Think again of the hippopotamus and the long number of page 19. Even if you have managed to create stories for all ten positions and 30 game cards with a lot of effort and time, these stories should have been quite boring.

And we tend to forget what is boring very fast, because it just does not impress us enough! So I think that now even the biggest doubters among you agree that we create our own pictures to our playing cards.

If you now believe that you have to memorize complicated pictures for each individual playing card, then I can becalm you. Because you have learned the playing card images you need for learning the technique – except for Ace of diamonds and Nine of clubs – already in our experiment with the keyframes!

I think that the principle of technology should now be clear to you. You will probably have one or two objections to the application of this technique. Believe me, these concerns will gradually dissolve into pleasure.

One of your biggest objections to the applicability of this technique may be that if you memorize several card games in sequence and repeatedly populate your body list with keyframes, you will eventually reach a point where you mess them up. Your objection is justified, of course. For this reason you will create several lists. Usually, eight different lists are sufficient for this.

If you think now that you have to memorize endless lists, I can becalm you. Firstly, you already have a list, and secondly, the other lists will be just as easy to learn as your body list.

You will also rehearse only positions that you already know with the other lists. In fact, you do not really have to learn anything at all, you just need to think a little bit - and only at the beginning!

Among other things, you will use your apartment or house with the individual rooms and their furnishings.

Perhaps your biggest objection is that you cannot imagine at the moment how your brain can process such long and imaginative stories in no time at all. This objection is indeed understandable from your current perspective, but unjustified! Also a short example for this:

Please think again of the foot story with the bulldozer!

What did you think of the word "foot story"?

You probably did not repeat the foot story word for word in your mind, but you only had one picture in your mind's eye.

A picture similar to a photograph showing a bulldozer driving a damsel at the wheel over her foot, pushing a bunch of bridal bouquets in front of her.

But when you read the "foot story" in history, it took about two or even three minutes because you had to "literally" read every detail.

You know, a picture is worth a thousand words!

Subject area four-colour card game

So that you can distinguish the individual colours values of the playing cards cleanly, simply and quickly when memorizing the cards, we will assign a subject area to each of the four colours:

Let us start with the colour value diamonds. We assign it the subject area knights and Middle Ages.

This topic has come to my mind, because in the present day the wooden shutters of medieval castles are often painted with red diamonds on a white background.

Granted, combining diamonds and the Middle Ages may be a bit unusual, but, as you already know, that is why it is easy to remember.

Unlike the colour value hearts. At hearts I certainly do not need to explain to you how love, marriage and happiness came to my mind.

Since the colour value spades is also referred to as a shovel or spade in some regions of Germany, I have assigned the topic construction site and work to this colour.

The colour value clubs has the shape of a cross and the cross symbolizes Christianity, including the topics church, death and burial.

Example queen of diamonds

Please think about which topic group or which colour value the castle damsel could belong to, who drove with the bulldozer over your foot (position 1 of your body list)?
Right, knights and Middle Ages, so you now know that the castle damsel must be a diamond playing card!
Furthermore, you know that the castle damsel is the second key image on your body list. Now, if you compare the second keyframe with the second card on your list of cards on page 140, then you also know that this is the colour value of the queen of diamonds!

Example queen of hearts

The colour value hearts has the theme of love, marriage and happiness. How do you think you could best visualize the queen of hearts?
I imagine a bride wearing the typical white wedding dress.

Can you still remember who in laborious work had scooped out all the sand from the sandbox on your shoulder (position 7 of your body list) with a concrete pipe?

Right again, it was the bride in the white wedding dress!

The queen of hearts has the card image of a bride!

Example queen of spades

Which lady would probably be emancipated enough not to leave the hard work on a construction site not only to the men?

Personally, the name Alice Schwarzer immediately comes to my mind. Do you remember that we have assigned the theme construction site and work to the colour spades?

Surely you also know which small and fast-paced story took place on your nose (the ninth position of your body list)?

If so, then you know that Alice Schwarzer was the third key in ninth position. She took the "whip" away from the squire, because he had hit the poor horses so terribly. The reason why this is our Queen of Spades and the 27th card on our card list as well as on the body list with your keyframes, you will now be able to understand yourself without difficulty, if you compare them!

Example queen of clubs

Where or as which playing card you now have to classify the reproachful widow of the knight, you may now come up with a little logic and consideration of your own.

Basically, it should be mentioned at this point that you do not necessarily have to borrow my pictures and topic suggestions.

Of course, you can also construct completely different images and subject areas.

Example animals

Let us suppose that you are currently studying zoology, for example, so you can prove the subject areas of the four colours as follows:

Diamonds = Insects, Hearts = Reptiles, Spades = Mammals and Clubs = Fish. Then the image for ace of clubs might be a shark, because it is among the fish at the top of the food chain.

What is important for our technology is not which images I give you, but what is important is that you can imagine these images crystal clear.

If you still have difficulties with one or the other picture, simply exchange it with another one.

On pages 143-174, I reserved a page for each of the 32 game cards in a pack of cards (French card game).

My interpretations of the playing cards with their respective subject areas can be found on the top half of the page in both written and graphic form.

If you have problems with the pictures given by me, you have the possibility for your own interpretations on the lower half of the page *.

Please get a card game now.

Colour diamonds

To begin our practical tasks, please first sort out all eight cards of diamonds - from seven of diamonds to ace of diamonds - from your deck of cards and put the remaining cards aside.

Make yourself as comfortable as possible, and try to do not get interrupted or disturbed during your exercises. Create a relaxed atmosphere for your exercises again, so you can fully use your mental performance.

* This does not refer to the replacement pictures; I will explain these later.

I ask you to think for yourself why you could associate diamonds with the theme of knights and the Middle Ages.

Take at least five minutes and try to imagine your associations as clearly as possible.

Here you can also incorporate arguments from our small stories that you had filed on your body list. If, for example, you are able to visualize the bulldozer-headed castle damsel in the forefront and automatically connect this image to the colour diamonds, it would be an argument why the colour diamonds are linked to knights and the Middle Ages.

These associations should be as clear to you as it is logical for you to keep your toothbrush in the bathroom and your cutlery in the kitchen and not the other way around! So you no longer have to consciously decide which topic group to assign to the colour diamonds.

If you're a very particular "left-brain" person, you might argue rationally: "I cannot do that!"

Motto: »How should I imagine something illogical as logical and self-evident?« In this case, I ask you to remember once again, for example, how you learned to drive a car.

If your car has a H-shift, it is perfectly logical for you today to have the first gear in the front left, the second gear in the back left, the third gear in the front right, and so on!

Furthermore, if your gear stick is in the middle at a distance of about 20 cm to your right thigh, then this seems completely logical! While driving you do not think in the least about where your gear stick is, in which gear you have to switch at which speed or where this gear is!

A humorous engineer

But let us imagine that your car was developed by a particularly humorous engineer and the gear lever is mounted behind the driver's seat. The first gear may then be in the back right, the second gear in the front left, the third perhaps half left in the middle and so on; that would be perfectly logical for you today. You would have learned it this way and not in another!

Hand on heart, how were your first driving lessons? Did not you have to think about where the different gears are?

Like the gears in your car, the subject areas of the colours and the visualization of your playing cards are stored with a little practice in your brain as a kind of standard picture world and retrieved completely automatically when required!

Now try to develop your own associations, why it could be logical that diamonds equate with knights and the Middle Ages! If you cannot cope with my depictions at all, then you have enough space on pages 143 to 150 for your own interpretations.

Own interpretations

Before you move on to the other colours with their subject areas, we continue with the illustration of the diamonds playing cards, because it is important that you train the individual colours with their subject areas and card images in the appropriate order.
If you now want to memorize your card images, so the stories that you have placed on your body list can be extremely helpful; you really do not have to learn the card images anymore, just remember them!
Again, of course, own interpretations are not only allowed, but even very desirable, because:

> Own and self-conceived pictures can be noticed faster and thus better than pictures given from the outside.

Start with the seven of diamonds (page 143, 24, key frame, position 8). It was the fearsome battle ax by which the bridegroom had smashed her yoke fastened to her neck.

When you have repeated this little story from the Middle Ages in your mind's eye again, you must have had a very specific picture of this noxious murder instrument, otherwise you would not have been able to experience this story mentally.

Your picture will certainly differ significantly from my picture of a battle ax. That is why I have listed a few examples of possible substitute images for each game card on pages 143 - 174.

What is meant by substitute pictures?

For example, supposing you remembered our "foot story", you saw an digger instead of a bulldozer, a princess instead of a damsel, and instead of the many bridal bouquets, you saw a single large pile of flowers in your mind's eye.

You may have unconsciously produced these slightly modified images because they were easier to remember for your brain. Despite the apparent mistakes, you reproduced our card images correctly and in the correct order, because:

> You would hardly confuse a damsel with a digger
> or a bulldozer with a princess!

Therefore, you should not limit yourself to a single and solid image for your playing cards, but let your imagination run wild:

Be creative with the pictures! Test which images are most "wholesome" for your brain, experiment what kind of images it likes (especially succinct) and which it does not like!

You will find that this "trial and error" is not only highly interesting, but also fun and highly effective memory training, because it requires your right brain!

It is very important that you take a lot of time for each and every card image. It is best to make these pictures in your head as if in slow motion, then decorate them with all your imagination and all your senses.

Produce with your imagination again moving, crazy and memorable pictures. To a delicate damsel, driving a stinking of exhaust fumes monster from a bulldozer with loud rattling chains, you will remember better than a normal driver sitting in his car.

Please also keep in mind that you must first produce only one picture for each card; individual variants or substitute images will come to your mind automatically!

> The more concise you produce your card images, the better and faster your card images will be later reproduced, so remember!

Please be sure to take your time, as this will make you learn the whole technology faster!

Your long-term memory

In any case, take a little break after each imagined and reproduced playing card image. Under certain circumstances, it may be that two information learned in quick succession inhibit each other in your long-term memory. Your long-term memory will continue to work - at least for a while - if you are no longer actively involved with the (previous) learning material!

Gradually, go through all eight diamonds cards in the manner described, until you believe that you can safely reproduce the individual card images from your memory without having to think twice. Please see pages 143 to 150 again, and add my own interpretations, if necessary.

Then mix your eight diamonds cards well, slowly open one card at a time, first tell the card image and then the corresponding card value.

At the same time, try to present one or the other card picture with its corresponding card theme, so that your pictures are anchored deeper into your memory with each additional exercise, until they can later be retrieved completely automatically, like the arrangement of the gears of your car.

Repeat this about eight to ten times. Then treat yourself with a little break. Then repeat this exercise three to five more times.

It is very important that you initially concentrate only on the colour theme and the corresponding card picture while practicing.

Practice without any additional time

If you want to continue the self-instruction for a long time after this exercise, you should repeat your card images, or even better the whole exercise, the following day. Further repetitions follow after 2, 4, 8, 16 and 32 days.

To save time, you can do a lot of exercises in situations where you only use your brain for physical functions, at times when you are usually bored.

Since these exercises can be performed without a card game - by means of your imagination - this training is also possible in the waiting room of a doctor, on the sunbed or during a tram ride at any time.

But please do not practice while driving, otherwise you may still see bulldozers on the road where there are not any. Or even worse, you think that the bulldozer coming from the right and thus right of way only holds for a ten of spades! If you pay attention to it, you will be amazed at how many situations arise in everyday life in which you can practice this technique without additional time, even if you just brush your teeth.

Make yourself comfortable now
and practice your first eight card images.

Colour hearts

Just as you have practiced with the eight cards of diamonds, please also proceed with the eight cards of hearts.

First of all, think again about why the colour hearts could have just the subject of love, marriage and happiness. Then please take extra time again to produce and reproduce your playing card images. Make yourself comfortable and focus on the colour theme of hearts. Make your own associations to the accompanying playing cards or fill my interpretations on pages 151-158 with your own creativity.

Faster data highways through practice

How do you succeed with your fantasy pictures in the meantime?
Probably a bit better than at the beginning of the book. That is why your previously idle brain regions and potentials are gradually beginning to form new nerve cells (neurons) or to create new connections with other neurons.
The neurons exchange information and data faster and faster via the nerve pathways (axons) using messenger substances (neurotransmitters) at their contact points (synapses).
Regular practice gives your brain an ever-expanding neural network, and the most common nerve tracts are wrapped in a kind of insulating layer (myelin), just like a power cable.
As a result, data travel up to 30 times faster than normal, so that your neural pathways, when fully developed and trained, function as fast information superhighways where information and data rush and race at unimaginable speed.

Nerve cell (neuron)

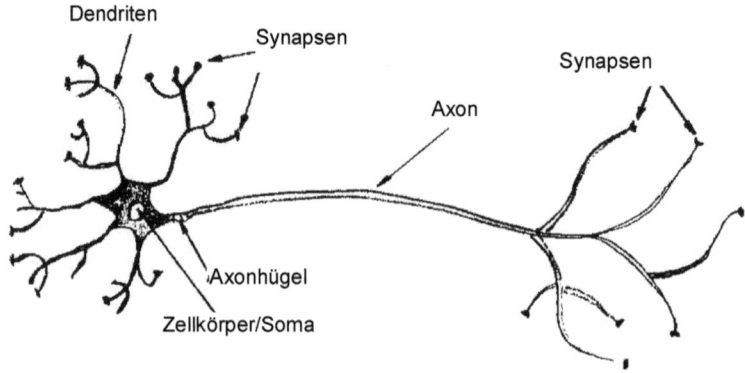

Dendriten

Synapsen

Synapsen

Axon

Axonhügel

Zellkörper/Soma

*Dendriten = Dendrite, Synapsen = Synapse,
Zellkörper = Cell body, Axonhügel = Axon hillock

If you want to synchronize your two halves of the brain (hemispheres), this is done via a kind of brain beam (corpus callosum). It also consists of a thick strand of nerve cell braids.

However, since these nerve cells (data highway) between your left and right hemisphere are still inexperienced, the data exchange that your two hemispheres need to convert abstract things such as map values into images, is still rather slow!

You are in the process of creating a trail that you will gradually expand into a fast information highway. As a result, this "image making" – like everything new you learn – is still relatively slow.

Remember how you learned to read!

At first, you had to laboriously learn each letter individually and then "puzzle them together" to finally understand the meaning of the word. And how do you read today?
Your eyes seem to capture only fragments of words or sentences as you read, because your brain's trained nerve pathways make these fragments perfect enough to recognize the other connections and understand the meanings, so that your eyes seem to scan the written lines.

Diamonds and hearts together

For the first half of your playing card values, you have now produced card images and believe you can reproduce these images effortlessly and quickly!? Then please take your eight cards of diamonds plus the cards of hearts and mix them well. Afterwards, please look at the individual cards one after another and pronounce the corresponding card image and the color values of the playing card aloud.
This will – in a similar way to the reading – go quite slowly in the beginning and of course, it depends on how well or less well you have produced your card images.
If you still have difficulties with a card picture, thus you hardly remember that card image, because you cannot imagine it crystal clear, then you should improve it mentally or exchange it with a completely different card image. Be sure to repeat this exercise until, after mixing and uncovering each card, you remember the card image faster than you can pronounce the actual card value.

I wish you a lot of fun and imagination while your exercises.

Spades and clubs

Before you start with the second half of your playing card images, I suggest that you also repeat the already learned card images and their meanings occasionally.

It goes without saying that all of our practical exercises and practice sessions can be spread over several days, weeks and even months, as long as you do not spend too much time between exercises or as long as you recapitulate what you have learned – at least at the beginning – once a day for a few minutes.

The frequency of repetitions depends on how long you interrupt our self-study or how much time you take for the exercises.

For the next one to two days, however, you can safely put aside your diamond and hearts cards to fully concentrate on the colours of spades and clubs.

Before you start with the second half of your playing card images, I suggest that you also repeat the already learned card images and their meanings occasionally.

It goes without saying that all of our practical exercises and practice sessions can be spread over several days, weeks and even months, as long as you do not spend too much time between exercises or as long as you recapitulate what you have learned – at least at the beginning – once a day for a few minutes.

The frequency of repetitions depends on how long you interrupt our self-study or how much time you take for the exercises.

For the next one to two days, however, you can safely put aside your diamond and hearts cards to fully concentrate on the colours of spades and clubs.

Congratulations!

I would like to congratulate you on the discipline and consistency with which you have followed these exercises so far! But also to your courage and your open-mindedness to try something completely new - so you stand out from the vast majority of your fellow human beings!

Let us recap in a nutshell the most important facts mentioned so far. Now that you know how your brain essentially works, you also know that it is extremely user-friendly for your brain to turn abstract information into figurative information. As a result, both hemispheres are synchronised and can cooperate with each other. Therefore, you have assigned all 32 (abstract) card values their card images, so that your brain can store the playing cards as brain-user-friendly as possible.

Furthermore, you know that this effect is still many times boosted, when you structure this information and data additionally.

Folders and positions

For the sake of simplicity, I now refer to these folders as lists. All in all, we will create ten lists of ten positions each for our game card memory technology - including the body list - so you can have more than one hundred positions in the future.

These lists of your positions are similar to your body list. Therefore, they will be just as quick and easy to learn, and they are even suitable for children.

Several lists are essential for our memory technique; otherwise you get confused with the map images and their order quickly.

Although our playing card memory technique would be enough for seven to eight lists, firstly, it does not hurt if you work out two or three lists as a reserve, and secondly you can use these lists and position combinations "ten times ten" – among other things with regard to your memory of numbers – accomplish still quite different startling memory achievements. Here I will give you some very interesting examples later, as well!

Before we begin to create the various lists, I would like to ask you to not neglect your already developed card images.

Every now and then take your card game to hand, mix it well, reveal the cards in a row and pronounce the corresponding card images or card values aloud. Or you repeat – if you do not have a card game at hand – your card values with the associated card images in mind.

A brilliant storage space

The benefit of this list method is that you can remember a hundred things as easily as ten.
Each of these lists, with their individual positions, effectively represents a storage space that can be reused or deleted over and over again, similar to a computer's memory or hard drive.
So these lists are probably the most effective way to remember almost unlimited things.
The quickest and safest way to create your lists is to populate them with familiar sequences and reference points.

Example:
Supposed, you drive to work every day by tram. So, after a while, you memorise the individual stops in their order. If you were to present photos of the stops and you would have to sort them in their order, you would not have any difficulties, even though you did not consciously acquire this knowledge.
In this case, you do not distinguish between the various stops by many details, but by very particular points.
For example, at the first stop, this could be a rusty dustbin, which annoys you every time because this ugly part completely disfigures the otherwise well-maintained stop.

At the second stop there is perhaps a particularly beautiful and well renovated half-timbered house, in which you would like to move.

So if you choose ten stops, at each stop you only need to remember one of those pithy things as a location for your "tram list" to have another watch list.

This way, you can search for significant points (positions) on all the roads or paths where you regularly ride, hike, or cycle, for creating new lists easily and quickly, whose orders you would certainly not mistake – without learning them for too long!

The place that is by far the most familiar to us and the one we visit most regularly is your own home. Therefore, the objects contained therein - as reference points - in their order and list as the easiest to remember. For this reason, we will link seven out of ten lists to your home - hereafter referred to as "apartment list"!

Place your apartment list with the positions 21 to 90 and your body list with the positions 91 to 100.

For the positions 1 to 10 and 11 to 20 I will suggest you two additional lists.

I will tell you later why the lists of your position numbers should be in exactly that order.

If you have difficulties with the application or composition of my list suggestions, please develop yourself one or two other lists. How this »list making« works and what you should be aware of is explained as we create the next two lists and your individual housing list.

A zoo in the skyscraper

The list of 1 to 10 consists exclusively of animals, since animals are usually seen as a very clear image and there is no great effort to mentally produce the corresponding images (think of the hippopotamus).

The order of the animals is arranged alphabetically by their first letters; this cannot be confused with the position number of the animals.

Now your imagination is in demand again.

I would like to ask you to imagine an unusual zoo.

Unusually, because this zoo was not created in a park-like landscape, but because it is in a ten-storey skyscraper.

Each of these floors has been developed and created for a specific species.

To help you remember the position number better, imagine that the monkeys (Apes, A = 1.) are performing a dart game using metal pins or nails instead of arrows, shaped like ones. So you do not only know from the alphabetical order that the Ape is the first position out of a total of 100 positions.

Of course, even without darts, it is clear to you that the letter "A" is the first letter in the alphabet! If, however, I ask you what the eighth letter in the alphabet is, then after a certain time (after you have counted all the previous letters) you can answer that question to me, but you would have spent a relatively large amount of time on it.

Not only are crystal clear images produced in your head important to the smooth operation of our technology, but it is equally important that you can assign these images to their positions with the associated numbers safely and, above all, quickly.

However, if you have to mentally count up and down all the previous positions, you can quickly end up with fast.

In addition, you now know that impossible, funny and crazy images with much "action" can be remembered much better than pictures that occur in everyday situations. Why not the monkeys playing with darts looking like "ones"?

Please try to experience these and subsequent descriptions and pictures as imaginatively as possible in your mind's eye.

If you look into the bear cage, you can see how the bear, with its unbridled strength, bends a straight iron bar about 2 cm thick into a "2"!

This monster chameleon does not eat any flies or other insects because of its enormous size, but is fed with its smaller mates, who are thrown into its cage.

As you watch the chameleon eating, you can see that it quickly blasts out of its mouth instead of the long sticky tongue a trident with barbs – as it is also used in fishing. It impales its fellows before it kills them.

You get a great dolphin show, in which an animal trainer holds a rectangular jump frame at a height of about 4 meters instead of a tire, so that not only one dolphin, but always four dolphins can jump synchronously next to each other.

Among these elephants also appears to be a deformed one, because one of the animals does not have two ears, but no less than "5".
One ear each on the right and left of the head, one like a shark on the back and one on the right and one on the left side of the butt.
Therefore, the elephant has also maliciously been given the name "a ... face" by the animal caretakers.
The poor animal looks more like an oversized coelacanth with a trunk.

> The 6th floor is shared by two hippos.
> The German word for hippopotamus = Flusspferd
> The 6th letter in the alphabet is F = 6.

Here you would rather not bother longer, because Mr. and Mrs. Hippo (Flusspferd, F = 6.) together provide for offspring and thus have sex (6).

> On the 7th floor the giraffes are trotting.
> The 7th letter in the alphabet is G = 7.

Looking at the giraffe's long neck and relatively small, angled head as a unit from the side, the appearance is reminiscent of the shape of a 7.

> On the 8th floor the hounds bark.
> The 8th letter in the alphabet is H = 8.

However, it is not normal dogs, but greyhounds racing among each other. For this purpose, there is also a dog track on the 8th floor, which is shaped like an 8 and reminiscent of an oversized slot car racing track.

> On the 9th floor you will see the poor hedgehogs
> The German word for hedgehog = Igel.
> The 9th letter in the alphabet is I = 9.

Poor hedgehogs (Igel, I. = 9.) because they are misused by their keepers as a conical ball, because on the 9th floor there is also a bowling alley by accident. The zookeepers always frighten the hedgehogs for their purposes until they curl up into a ball. With the "Hedgehog Ball" the orderlies try to hit all nine (9 cones).

On the 10th floor there is the jeti.
The 10th letter in the alphabet is J.

Due to the enormous rarity of jetis, the zoo was lent only one creature by the Buthan government, which is why the jeti is always boring because of its loneliness. So he crouches unmotivated in his corner and alternately sucks his ten toes (10) instead of his thumb.

The floors in the overview

Skyscraper Zoo	Alphabetic character	Animal	Characteristics
10th floor	J	Jeti	Alternately sucks his ten toes (10)
9th floor	I	Igel hedgehogs	Hedgehog is abused as a cone ball
8th floor	H	Hound	Hound is running on an eight-shaped racetrack
7th floor	G	Giraffe	Giraffe neck and head look like a seven
6th floor	F	Flusspferd Hippos	Hippo has sex (like 6)
5th floor	E	Elephant	Elephant with five ears (a ... face)
4th floor	D	Dolphin	Four dolphins jump side by side through a square frame
3rd floor	C	Chameleon	Chameleon has a trident instead of a tongue
2nd floor	B	Bear	Bear bends iron bar to a two
1st floor	A	Ape	Ape plays with the dart looking like a 1

As with your card images, think of replacement pictures again. Please practice the list until you know exactly – without thinking too much – which animal is in the same floor and what it is busy with at the moment.

Basically, it is easy to remember this list in its order. Everything important has already been stored in your memory. So you know from an early age how the animals you want to remember look like (apart from the jeti), so you do not have to produce images for these animals – in contrast to our card images.

Furthermore, the names of the animals are not unknown to you, and so you know with which initial letter or in which alphabetical order the animals are to be classified on the list.

All the facts taken together mean that you do not have to learn this »animal« list first, but only have to think imaginatively about their composition.

Nevertheless, in this case too – as with the card images – you should be slow and careful.

Try to bring the individual images and situations to life with all your imagination. And please repeat your card images a few times before returning to the book.

Hand on heart (brain)!

Did you really do all the previous exercises and practice sections exactly as they were described by me?

Do you know all card images with the corresponding card values from the bottom up, so that when you uncover a playing card, you can think of the card image faster than you can pronounce the card value?

Can you now say, without much thought at which position the letter H is placed within the alphabet?

To what extent you have understood everything so far and how disciplined you have done your exercises, you can test after the next break by daring your first attempt to memorise 30 playing cards.

I will explain later why we only use 30 playing cards at the beginning. Only this much in advance: If you follow this self-study only halfway seriously and with not too big interruptions, you can memorise 300 cards and more in their order by this technique!

Of course, due to lack of practice, you can not automatically recall the zoo list of your subconscious, but with a little thought, you should at least access that list out of your memory.

The same certainly applies to some of your card images. So you will need a lot of time in the beginning to memorise all 30 game cards in their order.

But your first attempts are not about speed or perfection, but about the fact that you will find that this technique really works!

If you have only 15 or 20 of the 30 cards right in your first try, please do not fret, just think back to how "many" cards you had correctly, as you tried to determine your card memory the playing card list from page 29.

Do the same with your first experiment as you did in the first experiment, except that you do not use your body list, but the zoo list.

The first time

For your first attempt to memorize playing cards, I recommend that you go into a learning environment where you have a table or other storage space within your reach.

Furthermore, you should again ensure that you are not disturbed during your exercise or otherwise interrupted in any way. Take as much time as you want, and do not put yourself under pressure. This is a self-study, so decide for yourself how much time you need for your experiment. And always remember:

The more unusual and noticeable your images are, the better you will be able to remember them, because these pictures literally imprint themselves. And the better you produce your stories and images, the faster your stories and images can be re-produced later!

If you think you have created all the prerequisites, you can start your first attempt with the following "Quick Start Guide".

Please read the following lines of the manual and the examples until the next pause sign at least once well and above all carefully before you start with the practical part of the exercise!

It is very important that you understand the content of the following instructions to 100 percent before you start with the practical part of the exercise!

Please take your card game and mix it well.

Hold the cards upside down as if you were about to hand out the cards. Lift the top card and place it face up on the table or any other tray.

Imagine the card image of this playing card as clearly as possible with all your senses and connect it mentally (with as much imagination as possible) with the image of the first position of your "zoo list", a monkey, monkey cage or whatever else you think of as a substitute image ,

As an example, let's take again the first story on our body list:

➢   Position 1 of our body list was the foot.
➢   The first playing card was the spades of 10.
➢   The map image for the spade 10 was the bulldozer.
➢   We had linked the card image of the first playing card (pik 10 = bulldozer) with the position 1 of the body list (foot), by imagining that this bulldozer with painful rattling drive chains and stinking diesel exhaust drives us painfully over the foot.

If you have linked the card image of your first playing card to the position image of the first position of the "zoo list" (monkey), please take the second playing card and place it face up on the first playing card. Please be especially careful here, otherwise the cards could mix inadvertently.

Now link as imaginatively and with all your senses the card image of the second playing card with the card image of the first playing card.

➢   In foot story, the second card was the queen of diamonds.
➢   The card image for the queen of diamonds was the castle damsel.
➢   Next we linked the card image of the second playing card (Queen of diamonds = castle damsel) with the card image of the first playing card (ten of spades = bulldozer) by picturing it like the delicate damsel with her blue silk dress and pointed hat would steer bulldozer.

Have you now securely linked the second card image to the first, and do you see all the previous links crystal clear in your mind's eye?

Do you experience the stories with all your senses? Then take the third playing card from your stack and put it back on the previous cards.

Link the third to the second card image or, if possible, even to both previous card images.

➢ In foot story, the third card was the nine of hearts.
➢ The card image for the heart of nine was the bridal bouquet.
➢ We had linked the third card image of the foot story with the second and first card image, imagining ourselves as imaginative as our second card image (castle damsel = queen of diamonds) using our first card image (bulldozer = ten of spades) huge heap of our third card image, the bridal bouquets (nine of hearts), pushes in front of him.

Please link the rest in the same way remaining 27 playing cards with the other nine positions your "zoo list".

If you still want to memorize the remaining two playing cards of your card game, you simply fill the 10th position of the "Zoolist" (Jeti) with a short story, which consists of five card shots instead of three.

As I said, please be sure to give yourself as much time as until you see the images and stories really crystal clear in your mind's eye.

After that, take your pile of cards (without accidentally mixing it) and turn it around so that the back of your cards is facing up and the first playing card you have memorized is back up.

Please take a sheet of paper and something to write.

Now try to write as many playing cards in the correct order as possible from your memory.

If you cannot remember one or the other card image, leave some space on your sheet of paper and proceed with your "zoo list"; the remaining cards may be assigned later. Then compare your notes with your deck of cards.

Important!

Please perform this experiment with your "zoo list" and the other newly learned lists only once! Doing this with the same list several times in a row would not only confuse you, it would also severely inhibit your mental capacity for our subsequent exercises, or even block it in the worst case! After learning all ten lists, you will be able to train this technique as often and as much as you want.

I wish you much fun and success in your first attempt!

What do you think about the number "11"?

If you have done all the previous exercises and instructions conscientiously, you will be thrilled with your own memory after this first attempt, and you are still completely untrained!!

In order to practice the technique again, we will now take care of putting together the list of positions from 11 to 20.

Since we only use reference points for our lists that are familiar to us, we will take advantage of the fact that our memory automatically associates certain things with certain numbers in the next list!

For example, what do you think about the number "11"? Please think about this number for a moment.

In my seminars, most of my participants associate the number »11« with soccer. This is also the name used by the German team in an international match "The German eleven", and everyone knows that the German football team is meant by the German team. Since the list below begins with position 11, we'll call it "football list" for the sake of simplicity.

If you think of football, even if you are not a soccer fan, you are sure to find a lot of images associated with this sport.

Such as soccer stadium, soccer field, soccer goal, soccer club, soccer player, soccer jersey etc. The more associations and substitutes (facets) come to your mind concerning this »soccer position« with the number 11, the easier and faster you can use this term to construct small stories.

What does a police car have in common with a nativity scene?

I would like to give you a little example:

Let us take the card image of the jack of clubs, the **nativity scene**.

What do you think a nativity scene - which usually radiates calm and comfort - could have in common with a police car that drove up because of a criminal hunt with a loud siren howl, glaring blue light and squealing tires?

Even after a long and thorough deliberation, you probably will not know what one might have to do with the other. I will explain the context to you: As you may have guessed, I have already spent a lot of time studying different memory and learning techniques before developing this self-study course.

Since I was not inexperienced in these matters, I felt that "making pictures" was too slow for some card combinations. If I want to imagine a nativity scene on my thigh, as in our "Thigh Story", then I can imagine this picture pretty much simply mentally.

On the one hand, I have the image of a crib - which affects the spatial proximity - directly in front of me (on my thigh), and on the other hand, I can imagine its weight on my thigh and so on.

However, if I had to imagine a nativity scene in our position 11 – let us take the soccer field as an example - I would not care less about this connection between the nativity scene and the soccer field because of the lack of spatial proximity and the not »perceived« weight.

Especially at the beginning you will also often experience that some card pictures and their combinations can only be combined very laboriously (and therefore time consuming) with each other.

> Therefore, it is very important that you are just starting to take a lot of time for these difficult shortcuts!

Hence, try changing your card- and position pictures in your mind's eye until you have them crystal clear. Your original card or positional image will not be unlearned, but the opposite is the case. You extend your images with many more valuable facets.

In this way, in my imagination, a police car was created as another facet of the nativity scene. First of all, I found it difficult to link it to my nativity scene on any position or card image, because the whole story would have been too ordinary and too boring.

Since one can usually not remember "ordinary" stories, I wanted to eliminate this "memory blockade".

So I thought about "sprucing up" the picture of the nativity scene by making it a bit "cheesy" to give it a little more dynamism.

Thinking of "cheesy", I spontaneously remembered the Venetian plastic gondolas from the 1960s and early 1970s, which were usually placed on the TVs with their small bright, colourful and flashing lights!

As a result, the nativity scene in my imagination was provided with these little flashy, blinking, colourful lights, and my problem was solved or rather enriched my card image with a first facet.

Another time, neither the ordinary nativity scene nor the cheesy crib would have been a good fit. Again, I thought briefly what you could construct from the bright, colourful and flashing lights of my nativity scene.

The result is another facet in the form of a flashing blue light with magnetic mount. A flashing blue light, as you get to see it in older American crime films, when the sheriff suddenly has to pursue a villain with his private vehicle and for this purpose from his glove box (already?!) flashing blue light takes out and using magnetic holder on his car roof placed.

It is logical that from the blue light one day a further facet in the form of a German police car with siren and squeaky tires had to develop automatically.

Surely you now understand why I have no difficulty in imagining a police car instead of a nativity scene on the card image of the Jack of clubs.

Even if I imagine a fire truck, because it can be particularly beautiful and above all quickly build into a story, I would know later while reproducing the story with certainty and without much thought that this is in fact the card image of the Jack off clubs (so the nativity scene)!

The likelihood of confusion with another card image is zero!

Because of the myriad possibilities of assigning more facets or substitute images to your already existing cards and positional images stored in your head, it is very important that you work with your images very slowly and concentratedly.

Every facet that you add to your pictures can, in turn, be linked to other facets simply and effortlessly, just as with a snowball effect.

The more facets you add to your pictures,
the more flexible and faster
you can produce new stories!

Twelve o'clock in the afternoon, High Noon

Back to the football list. The position 11 (football) should be clear so far, so that we continue now with the other positions.

> ## 12 = Cowboy

We associate the number 12 with the noon time, so that you can also think of the Western Classic (High Noon), which has already been broadcast countless times on German television under the title »12 Uhr Mittags«.

So you can tie everything together with the 12, which can be associated with wild west movies, cowboys, etc. This may include a saloon with its lightly clad female staff as well as a horse-drawn car or an old stagecoach.

But also famous characters or actors from well-known western series, such as Bonanza, which we have seen so often flicker across the screen.

13 = Chimney sweeper

If we look at the number 13, the optimists of you may rather think of a lucky number. But since luck and bad luck are very close to each other, you can combine lucky symbols such as chimney sweeps, lucky pigs, lucky pennies, etc. with the number 13 as well as pitch symbols, such as the black cat that can cross your path.

14 = Airplane

If one flies with the airplane on vacation, then one estimates for this project usually a period of 14 days. I propose that position 14 be linked to your memories of past air travel and I am sure that I will not have to help you with sample images at this point.

15 = Cake

At position 15, just think about the time. On Sundays at 15 o'clock, it is the time for coffee and cake for many. Even if you only enjoy a few coffee gossips a few times a year, you have probably stored some pictures of such an event in your memory.

For example, imagine grandma's old, valuable coffee service or cakes and pastries of all kinds. If you regularly take part in a coffee gossip or organise one and there are always the same people involved in it, so you could also include this in your "cake pictures".

If you prefer to spend your sunday at 3pm in a cozy wine bar to maybe play a game of skat, you will not find it difficult to turn the proposed images into other ones.

16 = Motorcycle

Position 16 is the motorcycle, because you can buy the license for a small motorcycle (also called moped) according to law until the age of 16 years. Again, do not limit yourself to the image of a single and specific motorcycle.

Think again as many, different and clear pictures. How about other two-wheelers, such. Bike, scooter, Harley Davidson, scooter, racing or sidecar motorcycle? Or you imagine your first bicycle or moped and try to remember what you experiences with it.

17 = Girl

In position 17 imagine a pretty girl or a young woman with blond hair. Why? I think even to the younger readers the evergreen »17 Jahr, blondes Haar« by Udo Jürgens should be well known.

As far as equal rights are concerned, readers should note that you can imagine a handsome young man with blond hair without any risk of confusing position 17 with one of the other positions.

18 = Soldier

At 18, young men in Germany not only come of age, but also conscripted. As a result, some of them are drafted into the army as soldiers. Associate position 18 with a soldier. Since a modern soldier also has to carry a large number of pieces of equipment around with him, you can once again come up with many substitute pictures that associate you with a soldier or his own army (army, air force, navy).

Perhaps you have also experienced situations – with or in the army – that have indelibly "buried" themselves in your memory. These pictures, which already exist for you, are also perfect!

19 = New Year's Eve fireworks

In position 19, we remember how we said goodbye during the new millennium party at the end of 1999 from the old millennium. You will probably have received the new year thousand with colorful New Year's Eve rockets.

Of course, images of other fireworks items such as snap-frogs, boulders, laburnums, etc. are also suitable. You could even let real missiles such as the Apollo rocket that has flown to the moon or rockets that were unfortunately not used for such peaceful purposes "hit" in your stories dynamically.

Do you know how many bottles of beer are in most beer boxes?
Correct! 20 bottles! So our position is 20 "beer".

In this picture you can literally incorporate your senses (pleasant or unpleasant) through smell and taste. Beer boxes and bottles of all kinds are suitable as pictures here as well as beer kegs, beer steins, beer pavilions, beer tents, etc. Again, you should try again to remember experiences or events that you can connect with this issue.

The football list in the overview

Position	Designation	Characteristics
11	Football	The German eleven - Football team
12	Cowboy	12 noon - The Western (High Noon)
13	Chimney sweeper	Lucky number 13 - Chimney sweep brings luck
14	Airplane	14 days holiday - The flight on vacation
15	Cake	Sundays at 15 o'clock - Coffee gossips
16	Motorcycle	16 years old - Driver's license for moped
17	Girl	17 Jahr, blondes Haar - Evergreen by Udo Jürgens
18	Soldier	At the age of 18 - Compulsory military service
19	New Year's Eve rocket	1999 to 2000 – New Year's Eve and New Millennium
20	Beer	20 bottles in the beer box

I have already given you some suggestions for substitute pictures, but you should also use your own creativity and come up with as many imaginative pictures as possible. Please practice the football list until you are convinced that you will be able to call it from your memory without difficulty.

Remember all 32 cards
in their order!

To do so, prove your position 20 of the football list (beer) with five instead of three card images. But remember, the better, the clearer and slower you produce your pictures and stories, the better, clearer and faster you can remember your pictures and stories later!

For your second try, if possible, please return to a place where you can sit comfortably, relaxed and above all undisturbed. Please also keep in mind that there is a table or other storage space near you.
Before you start, please read the following instructions (until the pause sign). Then take your well-mixed card game, hold it up with the back of the card and reveal the first playing card. Get back into the role of the scriptwriter by using all your imagination to make the card image of the playing card appear in your mind's eye and mentally match the image of the first position on the football list (football) or one of the substitute images that you choose for it Position, link.

If you have linked the card image of the first playing card to the position image of your first position, please take the second game card and place it face up on the first card. Now link the card image of the second game card with the card image of the first game card.

You think you have safely linked the second card image to the first one? You see all previous links crystal clear in your mind's eye or experience them with all your senses?
Then take the third playing card from your stack, put it back on the cards you have already revealed, and then link the third card to the second, or if possible, to both previous card images.

Then, in the same way, link the remaining 29 playing cards to the other nine positions on your football list.

Be sure to allow yourself enough time to see and experience the pictures and stories crystal clear in your mind's eye. And please keep in mind that you should only do this once with your football list and the other newly learned lists!

I wish you a lot of fun and success with your second try!

A great sense of achievement

Nice that you are back! You probably had a great sense of achievement again this time !?
The beauty of this memory technique is that you can not only reproduce the sequence of the individual playing cards, but also tell which playing card was drawn or how many!

Attention!
If you have a dislike of anything remotely related to math, please skip the following text (until the next pause sign). The following calculation examples are not important for the actual map memory technology. I wish all mathematics enthusiasts a lot of fun in mental arithmetic!

What was the 186th playing card?

Since we always occupy our lists with 10 main positions and each main position is again occupied by 3 card pictures (sub-positions), we have 30 card pictures or sub-positions on each list.
Compared to fraction calculation, one could say that each list contains 10/1 (10 whole) main positions or 30/3 (30 thirds) sub-positions.

As an example, if you take a look at our list of bodies with their card layouts (foot history, etc.) and you would be asked what the 9th playing card on this list is, you would probably think for a moment and remember that the 9th card image The Bible is, therefore, as the third subheading on your third main position, your thigh. Since the Bible is the card image for the Ten of clubs, you know,

That the 9th game card is the Ten of clubs.

They needed only 3 x 3 = 9 or 9 : 3 = 3 to count.
Since there are 3 sub-positions in the form of card images associated with each main position on their body list, you know that all sub-positions that are numerically smoothly divide by 3 are the last sub-position = card image = game card in the respective main position.
You will find the 30th card (30: 3 = 10) as the last card image (sub-position in the form of a flag) on the last of the 10 main positions (the hair) of your body list.

This is the Nine of diamonds.

You will find the 21st game card (21: 3 = 7) as the last card image (Concrete Pipe / Eight of spades on your 7th main position (the shoulders), etc.

These mathematical examples may not have been too difficult for a mathematical enthusiast. If so, please do not fret, just skip this chapter and try again. (As already mentioned, this chapter is not absolutely necessary for the application of our memory technique.)
*
It gets a bit more difficult with the sub-positions, which can not be divided smoothly by the number 3. To determine these sub-items, you must use the fraction calculation.
For example, if you want to know what the 7th card on your body list was, you must count 7: 3.
The result is then 2 and 1/3.

So you come to 2 full main positions (feet and knees) with 3 sub-positions (2 x 3 = 6) plus the 1st sub-position (map image) (1/3) of the 3rd main position, so this is the 1st sub-position (card picture) on the 3rd main position (thigh).

- ➤ The third main position was the thigh.
- ➤ The first card picture or the first sub-item was the nativity scene.
- ➤ The card image nativity scene stands for Jack of clubs.

The 7th playing card was Jack of clubs.

Next, you may want to know what the 20th playing card on your body list was.

Divide 20 : 3. As a result, you come to 6 and 2/3.

So on 6 full main positions (6 x 3 = 18) plus 2 subpositions or card pictures (2/3) of the 7th main position.

- ➤ The 7th main position was the shoulder.
- ➤ The 2nd card picture or 2nd subposition was the bride.
- ➤ The card image of the bride is the Queen of hearts.

The 20th playing card was Queen of hearts.

You do not need to recalculate the fact that the 19th playing card was Jack of Spades (Sandbox) or the 21st playing card Eight of Spades (Concrete Pipe).

*

Suppose you were much further away with this book, had ten different lists and wanted to remember 300 playing cards in their order. So you would have to occupy all 10 lists and their 10 main positions with 3 card images.

For example, if you want to know what the 186th game card is, then reckon with

186: 3 = 62.

Then you know that these are 6 full lists and 2 full main positions!

As reminder

We have full major positions when a number (such as 186) can be easily divided by the number 3.

6 lists x 10 main positions = 60 main positions.
Each of these 60 main positions has 3 sub-positions or card images:
60 main positions x 3 sub-positions = 180 sub-positions / playing cards

+ 2 full main positions on the 7th list:
2 main positions x 3 sub-positions = 6 sub-positions / playing cards

Result = 186 sub-items / playing cards

With the facts you already know, this bill would look like this:

Assuming that our list of bodies is this 7th list, our foot would no longer represent the 1st main position (as in our other examples), but it would be our main position 71, our knee would then be main position 72, thigh 73, and so on.

Since each of the 3 sub-positions in a main position represents a card image, which in turn corresponds to the card value of a playing card, and you want to know which was the 186th playing card, all you have to do is remember what card image you are 3rd and last (3rd sub-position) on your 2nd main position with your 7th list. Because our 7th list is our body list in this calculation example, then the 2nd main position would be our knee!

➢ On our knee we first had the incredibly fat and screaming baby, so the Jack of heart (184th playing card).
➢ Second, we had the earth hoe with which this baby repeatedly hit the head. That was the Seven of spade (185th playing card).
➢ On the last (the 3rd) subposition of our knee was the hard hat that you put the baby on its head for self protection.

Since the hard hat was our card image
for the King of spades,
he is also our 186th playing card
in this calculation example.

If you have followed and even enjoyed the mathematical section of our self-study course, I recommend that you design and practice some of your own arithmetic from time to time.

However, if you want to use our card-memory technique mainly to know which cards have already been played during a card game, then it does not matter to you if the card was the 32nd or the 186th!

On the other hand, such knowledge can certainly have its attractive sides, for example if you consider the following situation:

In the casino

Imagine being in a casino. As you are more interested in blackjack than in roulette, sit down at a gaming table where some people are playing. One of your table neighbors ponders loudly about whether the ace of spades has already fallen or not. They make it clear to him (so that the croupier can hear it too) that the ace of spades is already in the 26th card.

You do not even believe what the croupier does for a "face" if you repeat this a few times and then ask him to give you cards, because you want to risk a game!

The use of mathematics in conjunction with the memory techniques of the 1st and 2nd chapter, your teammates would certainly be funny. The casino operator probably not!

Therefore, always behave as inconspicuously as possible at the gaming table.

Your apartment list (individual characteristics)

Let's move on to our last and longest list, the apartment list on which positions 21 to 90 are located.
The apartment list is basically the same as the example of the tram stops on the way to your work, which I have already given you.

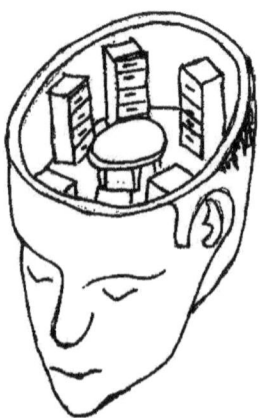

These types of lists are also called route lists, because you mentally a fixed route with its fixed in the order route points (for example, striking things or objects) steps off or leaves.
It is very important that you always build your routes according to the same pattern so that you can find these route points (positions) as quickly and safely as possible.
If your position points are in rooms as in our apartment list, you should always walk along the wall from left to right (or the other way round) in these rooms, or you can look around the room in a clockwise direction from left to right (or the other way round) ,
When things are in a room on top of each other, you should always arrange the bottom in front of the top position (or the other way round) first.
Whether you decide from left to right or from right to left or from bottom to top or vice versa, the position points in their order is up to you ...

... It is important that you always keep the same order!

Only then will you be able to use your memory at any point in your route without running the risk of confusing on the left with the top right or bottom with the top.

Since you have only occupied your body list, the zoo list and also the football list with only 10 main positions, you are now sure to wonder why we have the housing list with 70 main positions. Quite simply, the apartment list is just the generic term for 7 more lists, each with 10 main positions. We will distribute these 7 lists to the individual premises of your dwelling.

Since I can not know how your apartment or house with the individual rooms and premises is divided, I have come up with a kind of fantasy apartment for you. Based on this fantasy apartment I will explain to you how you can easily create an individual housing list - which then matches your actual environment.

Since the fantasy apartment is a very normal four-room apartment with kitchen, hallway and bathroom, I hope that my apartment designed for you may resemble your actual dwelling a little bit.

On page 120 you will find a graphic representation of this apartment and rooms for your own entries.

The 7 lists of our apartment list correspond to one room
and are arranged as follows:

1st floor =	Positions 21 to 30
2nd living room =	Positions 31 to 40
3rd kitchen =	Positions 41 to 50
4th dining room =	Positions 51 to 60
5th office =	Positions 61 to 70
6th bedroom =	Positions 71 to 80
7th bathroom =	Positions 81 to 90

If your apartment is smaller than the imaginary apartment that I have designed, then instead of the proposed room, for example, take your cellar, garage, storage, garden, workstation, train stops or the like as a substitute.

There are countless ways in which you can easily create lists that can then be populated with familiar items in a unique order for you. For example, if you do not have an office or study in your premises, delete the term on page 120 and simply replace the "office list" with another.

When creating your apartment list, you will proceed in a similar way as you already did when you created your body list. Here you have 10 reference points on your body, for example, to link the individual products of a shopping list with these.

You will notice very quickly that the composition and order of your apartment list - despite the many positions - can be quickly and easily memorized with a few small user strategies. Because your premises with the things in them are already known and trusted in their order!

Spatial order

To give you a first example of how you can create room lists with your apartment, I would like to describe the approach to you on the basis of my own kitchen.

For this you need to know that I put my fixed points - in their spatial order - basically from left to right (clockwise).
For fixed points, which are arranged above or below each other, I always start with the lower one.

While I am describing my kitchen, I would like to ask you to present my remarks as pictorially as possible.

When I enter my kitchen, I see on the left side first about a two-meter-high refrigerator combination, are stored in the mostly food.
The first main item on my kitchen list is the food refrigerator.
If I continue on my left wall, then I see two succinct things there.

On the one hand there is an electric stove, which is equipped with four hobs and an oven, on the other hand, an extractor hood, which is conveniently mounted above the electric range at an appropriate distance from the hobs.

As I always put the lower fixed points in the list first in my spatial order, the electric range is my second and the extractor hood the third main item on my list of kitchens.

A little further along the left wall is a stainless steel sink that consists of a sink with a dish rack and is my fourth reference point.

And finally there is a coffee machine on the left wall on a worktop. She is my position 5.

Please try - very slowly - the first five positions
and to visualize their sequence:

> ➢ Position 1 = Refrigerator
> ➢ Position 2 = Electric stove
> ➢ Position 3 = Extractor hood
> ➢ Position 4 = Stainless steel sink
> ➢ Position 5 = Coffee machine

If I continue on my kitchen route clockwise, next comes the headboard of the kitchen. Since this wall is also the outer wall of the house, there is a large window there, which is very concise for me at first.

The radiator below the window could at first glance make a nice fixture. Both things would be quite suitable as position points, but have the disadvantage that almost all rooms are equipped with a window and a radiator.

To avoid confusion with other positions, you should not use positions with the same name more than once. Even if you are absolutely sure that you can distinguish your kitchen window from the window in the living room. Instead, choose things that are typical of the room. It is even better if you find reference points that can not be found in another room.

For example, think of positions 2, 3 and 4 in my kitchen. Where else is there a stove with extractor fan or a stainless steel sink?

That's why I chose the trash can as the sixth position on the headboard of my kitchen.

If I continue my kitchen route in a clockwise direction, I come to the right wall and see a table there. But since a table could be in almost all rooms, this is not typical for a kitchen enough for me. The situation is different with the toaster that is on this table. The toaster is my seventh position.

Next up, in position 8, is a multifunctional kitchen machine that will not only crush all sorts of vegetables and fruits, but also cause hellish noise.

Position 9 is an antique two-piece kitchen buffet made of softwood, whose small doors are provided with leaded glazing.

Next to the kitchen buffet is my drinks refrigerator. But since I already have a food refrigerator in my first position and would like to rule out any likelihood of confusion, I have selected as position 10 my microwave oven, which is located on the drinks refrigerator.

All ten items summarized in my kitchen:

> Position 1 = Refrigerator
> Position 2 = Electric stove
> Position 3 = Extractor hood
> Position 4 = Stainless steel sink
> Position 5 = Coffee machine
> Position 6 = Trash can
> Position 7 = Toaster
> Position 8 = Food processor
> Position 9 = Kitchen buffet
> Position 10 = Microwave

Please try to visualize all ten positions in my kitchen with the corresponding spatial order. Afterwards, you may treat yourself to a short coffee break and then try to replay my kitchen list from your memory.

Room-typical objects

I do not think you have had a particularly hard time reproducing my list of kitchens from your memory, although in truth you have never seen my kitchen with the objects in it and therefore do not even know it!

What do you think about how easy it will be to remember when you create lists in your own familiar premises using the items you already know?

I would like to return to the room-typical objects such as cooker, extractor hood, etc. In my own apartment list, more specifically in my living room, I have made an exception.

Since my grandfather was a gifted architect and painter, I decorated almost all the rooms of my apartment with oil paintings, watercolors or drawings of him. The most beautiful pictures in my opinion, of course, have found their place of honor on the walls of my living room.

When I "tinker" my living room list, I noticed that the number of pictures that are exactly at eye level coincidentally gave the number 10. So I assigned a position to each of these 10 images.

Now you could rightly object that this creates a high risk of confusion with other images in other rooms, think of the example with the window and the radiator in my kitchen. But first of all, I'm limited only to pictures that my grandfather painted, secondly only to those that hang in my living room at eye level, and third - that's crucial - I associate each of these pictures with very different things, places or situations (substitute pictures).

Example:

The fifth position in my living room is a picture that essentially shows a river with a bridge. As one of my hobbies is fishing, I associate this picture with my favorite setting, which I have visited at least a hundred times. Thus, the image of this fishing spot is immediately and crystal clear in my mind's eye when I think about it.

In the eighth position of my living room is a picture whose main theme is a church.

I associate this picture with Cologne Cathedral and its surroundings. Although I have only seen or entered the Cologne Cathedral up close seven or eight times, those of you who only once had the privilege to visit this building will certainly agree with me if I say:

This picture is so impressive that you will not forget it so fast.

Believe me, that I can be one hundred percent sure not to confuse Cologne Cathedral with my favorite place of fishing!

Please be careful not only when choosing the things you choose for your apartment list, but try

You also fathom what you can associate with these things. First select the most impressive things for you for your positions or reference points.

However, before you start choosing positions individually, you should be clear about which room you are starting with. In our fantasy apartment, as you can see from the graphic on page 120, I chose the hallway first because this is the first place you enter after opening the front door.

Positions 21 to 30 of our fantasy apartment are in the hallway.

You too should arrange your housing list in a specific order.
Choose the order in which you would enter these premises, for example, during an apartment visit.

This is very important in the housing list at the beginning because of the many positions, so that you can better and more quickly remember the order of the rooms after creating the list.

An additional and excellent guide is to organize your rooms by name and number, for example by linking the apartment lists to the animals of your zoo list.

Orientation guide

I would like to give you some helpful examples (no math!): Your housing list is divided into seven main lists (rooms). Each of these seven main lists is again divided into ten positions. There are a total of seventy positions in your list of flats.

The numbering of the main positions starts (in our example) with the first position of the corridor list, with the position number 21, and ends on our bathroom list with the position number 90.

On each list, nine out of every ten numbers start with the same starting number. The starting number of the corridor list is the number 2.
The first nine numbers or positions are: 21, 22, 23, 24, 25, 26, 27, 28 and 29.
From this "initial number rule" always deviates only the last number of a list, and that is the number with the 0 at the end. In the corridor list it is the number 30!

If you want to use your zoo list as - in the truest sense of the word - small guide to the housing list, follow these steps:

The bear is on the second floor on your zoo list. You remember?
The bear starts with the letter B, the second letter in the alphabet. In order to better and more quickly remember the location numbers of your housing list, you might imagine that your entrance to the corridor is guarded by a grim and snarling bear.

Or you imagine that every time you come home and enter your apartment, a happy excited bear comes running down the hall instead of a dog, who licks your face with his tongue out of sheer joy of reunion.

To be able to better orient yourself at the beginning, simply call your corridor list a "bear corridor list". Since you have already linked the bear to the number 2 in your memory, you automatically know that all numbers - except for the last one - start with your "initial number" 2 on your bear corridor list!

For example, your living room (positions 31 - 40) could be renamed as a "chameleon room" because the chameleon is in the 3rd position of your zoo list (Chameleon = C = 3rd letter in the alphabet) and the first nine Starting from ten position numbers in your chameleon room with the number 3.
To better memorize the new name for your living room, you might imagine that every time you enter your living room, you'll be angry with a three-meter-tall and poisonous green chameleon.

In your kitchen (positions 41 - 50) your sink could turn into a dolphinarium (dolphin = D = 4th letter in the alphabet).
For this, you could imagine that when you enter your kitchen you are always greeted by a happy and loudly chattering dolphin, who splashes you every time with his Fluke from top to bottom.

When you enter your dining room (positions 51-60), you may imagine, like a little elephant with 5 ears (elephant = E = 5th letter in the alphabet) on your dining table, standing on its hind legs, with its big trunk golden ball balanced.

In your office (positions 61 to 70), you may see a cigar-smoking hippopotamus (hippopotamus = N = 6th letter) in your mind's eye, curling around in your desk chair and not having any offspring problems in the near future because Mr. Hippopotamus can now leave everything else to Mrs. Hippopotamus.

When you enter your bedroom (positions 71 to 80), you might imagine a giraffe (giraffe = G = 7th letter in the alphabet), which has a white apron studded with lace and a pink duster in its mouth high bedroom cupboards for you dust wipes. Because of its long neck, the giraffe naturally has a much easier time with this job than you.

For example, in your bathroom (positions 81-90), imagine a 100-pound St. Bernard (dog = H = 8th letter in the alphabet) sitting in your bathtub wearing a captain's cap on his head, using his root brush Scrub your back while belching loudly, because he has drunk far too often from the keg that hangs around his neck.

These little stories, of course, are meant to serve as examples of how to easily orient within such a long list, and to once again encourage you to invent your own little stories.

If you use your zoo list as an orientation list, not only does it have the advantage for you - especially at the beginning - within your housing list, that you can better orientate yourself, but at the same time it strengthens and trains the order and composition of your zoo list!

Sketch a floor plan

➢ To get started with your apartment list, first get a sheet of paper, a pencil and an eraser.

➢ Sketch the floor plan of your dwelling, or use the graphical representation on page 120 instead of a sheet.

➢ Next, please specify the order in which you would enter or visit the premises of your home.

➢ Give each room of your apartment list a name and enter it on your sheet of paper or in your book.

➢ Number each room list according to the scheme I presented on page 110, ie the first room from 21 to 30, the second room from 31 to 40 and so on to the last room, which you then number from 81 to 90.

➢ Determine in which spatial order (Sequence) you want to arrange the objects on your lists, whether from left to right or from right to left and from bottom to top or from top to bottom.

For the sake of simplicity I will explain the following procedure according to my scheme - from left to right and from bottom to top - and the same room names and item numbers as shown in the example graphic on page 120.

Example graphic for an apartment list

Kitchen 3 Dolphinarium	Hallway 1 Bear - kennel	Living room 2 Chameleon terrain
41. 42. 43. 44. 45. 46. 47. 48. 49. 50.	21 22 23 24 25	31. 32. 33. 34. 35. 36. 37. 38. 39. 40.
Office 5 Hippo enclosure	Hall	**Dining room 4** Elephant area
61. 62. 63. 64. 65. 66. 67. 68. 69. 70.	26 27 28 29 30	51. 52. 53. 54. 55. 56. 57. 58. 59. 60.
Bathroom 7 Doghouse		**Bedroom 6** Giraffes - cages
81. 82, 83. 84. 85. 86. 87. 88. 89. 90.	Genial Gemerkt	71. 72. 73. 74. 75. 76. 77. 78. 79. 80.

Fixing and numbering

Please enter your hallway (or the room you have selected as the first room in your list of flats) and let your eyes slowly turn 360 degrees clockwise. Or just turn slowly from left to right around your own axis.

Search for ten key points in your hall and inside the "circle" and number them in their order of 21 to 30. Again, think back to what criteria I used when creating my kitchen list have proceeded.

For example, if you look to your left in your hallway and see a key box after entering the apartment, this key box could be the first waypoint on your home list. In this case, you can write down the key box on your sheet or in the book as your position number 21.

As mentioned earlier, you should try to find room-typical things or objects as possible route points for the different rooms. Since a key box is usually mounted in the hallway, it could be an easy to remember (typical room) route point.

Now, if you let your eyes wander in a clockwise direction, you might next see a coat rack where you can hang your coat, jacket, or hat after putting your keychain in the key box. This wardrobe would then be in order of your position number 22.

Next, you'll see your answering machine, with new messages stored on it, as you can tell by the flashing light. So you would probably listen to your messages. Your answering machine could therefore be your position number 23, etc.

Give yourself plenty of time again and try to figure out why you chose these items as your position points (waypoints). Think about what experiences, situations or experiences you associate with these items. Try to find out now which substitute images you could associate with these waypoints. Just as I did with my river and bridge picture (= favorite fishing spot).

The more intensively and consciously you choose your route points, the better and faster you will be able to memorize them.

If you have decided on a route point, please fix and number it in writing in the appropriate place on your sheet or in the book.

Before you begin with the next room, once or twice you mentally leave your route points and then try - after about 5 to 10 minutes - to repeat your corridor list with the associated position numbers in their order.
Only then do you start with your other premises.

Note:
Please do not try to immediately show card images of your newly created corridor list! That would be easily possible, but it would distract you unnecessarily from the procedure for creating the housing list that you have just "read"!
Instead, just focus on your list of flats until you have created them - if possible in one piece - completely. If you follow this suggestion, you'll be amazed at how quickly and easily you can memorize your total of 70 route points in their order.

Tip:
For the initial handling of your lists, I also recommend you to always mark the 5th position number of the respective list - for faster orientation - with your hand (has 5 fingers) mentally.

Example:
On the 5th position of our zoo list are the elephants.
Elephants are known to trumpet loudly with their proboscis.
Imagine that you touch the 5th position of your body list with the 5 fingers of your hand and thus a deafening compressed air trumpet is set in motion!
Or you imagine again the 5th position on my kitchen list (coffee machine): If you touched the associated hot glass jug with your hand, you would terribly burn your 5 fingers, etc.
Again, be sure to invent your own stories and versions!

Practice creates masters

You have now worked out all 10 lists with 10 positions each.

- ➢ The zoo list with the positions 1 to 10
- ➢ The football list with positions 11 to 20
- ➢ The apartment list with the positions 21 to 90
- ➢ Your body list from 91 to 100

Thus, you have created 100 folders in your brain that you can fill as needed with playing card images or other information and data. From now on you can start with your regular card training.

Always occupy your 10 lists one after the other with your card images. To do this, start with your zoo list and continue with the (numerically) list below, in order to better memorize the individual lists with their fixed points and their sequence with each further exercise.

Of course, remembering playing cards will initially be relatively slow. Think back to how laboriously you learned to read. You may also remember what your first driving lessons were like.

These are some examples of how your brain works for you automatically today, as it has created fast data highways for these actions and activities. You know that only through continuous practice can ever more extensive neuronal patterns arise, and these enable the neurons to exchange data faster and faster.

The same is true of the card memory technology. Before the self-study, you probably have not thought it possible for you to remember a complete card game in sequence, let alone say where in the right place which card is.

Therefore, you should train and develop your knowledge and your newly acquired skills accordingly. Whenever possible, spend about 20 to 30 minutes each day building your information superhighway by linking your map images to your lists in the way I describe them.

If possible, practice at the same time every day, so that you reserve a specific time slot for your own personal brain jogging. Practice slowly and wisely, especially at the beginning, using all your imagination in the related stories.

You will see that this expenditure of time pays off especially in card games where certain card values or colours must be served, such as. Skat, Black Jack, Poker, Bridge, etc., because in such games very specific combinations of cards are constantly repeated.

Example: Skat

Suppose you currently have the game and cross is trump. One of your opponents got the last trick and now plays with the King of Diamonds because he believes that his opponent has the 10 of diamonds and you still have the 8 of diamonds.

Your second opponent now actually serves the King of Diamonds with his diamond 10, because he also believes that you still have the diamond 8.
Regrettably (for your opponents) you have "down" the diamond 8 and to the horror of your opponent trump the now important 14 points with your Queen of clubs!

> The order of the cards played was:
> King of Diamonds, 10 of Diamonds and Queen of Clubs!
> Expressed in card images: Knight, Lance and Widow!

Do you notice anything about this card image combination?
Just try to remember the story I told you about your 4th position (buttocks) on the body list!

In memory of:

What comes to your mind spontaneously when I ask you now whether you can sit down without problems and above all painlessly in the meantime? It probably reminds you of the dramatic story that took place in your position 4, the butt.
Who was responsible for the whole dilemma? Of course, the knight! That knight in his shining armor and galloping horse who attacked you for absolutely no reason when you were actually enjoying your lovely walk.
Surely you still remember the pain and the weapon with which the knight so accurately stabbed you in the butt?
Exactly! With his lance!

And what happened to the knight after stabbing with his lance?

His horse stumbled, and the knight fell headlong on the sidewalk, clanking his armor, bending his metal cap so hard that he broke his neck and died.

Your pain has now become so severe that you have become unconscious. When you came to, you saw the widow of the knight, dressed in black and telling you that she was a widow because of you.

> The keywords on your position 4, the buttocks, were:
> 1st = knight - 2nd = lance - 3rd = widow

If you have followed this self-study so consistently and experienced every story that I thought up for you at least once in your mind's eye, then this story should also immediately be pictorial in your memory, namely:

> ! As a single overall picture !

This means that you do not need to think up a history for this combination of cards, because - as with your card images - you have already saved a complete picture in your memory.

Always assuming you have taken the time to recapture this little story with all your imagination, senses, and feelings, and have made it as crazy as possible.

As you can see, it is very important at the beginning that you take a lot of time for these exercises in order to anchor in your memory the lists that are completely new to you, the card images and their combinations as concisely and strangely as possible.

So that you - with appropriate exercise - the desired memory not only quickly, but even with a certain automatism retrieve from your memory. Once you have reached this phase due to regular practice, you will gradually have to invent fewer and fewer stories on each of the map images.

Instead, you will be stacking more and more fixed images stored in your head in your subconscious mind so you can remember exactly which playing card was played and when and how many cards were played!

You can then compare this with "scribbling" when making a phone call.

MLS method
Michael Lutz System ©

So far, you have - apart from the playing cards substitute pictures - assigned a playing card image to each playing card value or a topic area for better orientation to the playing card colors.

Since you should now be familiar with your playing card images and easily assign them to the playing card values and playing card colors, I will now introduce an extension of the previous technique, which builds on my previously described system.

Although this method is initially more complicated and time-consuming, it has the advantage that the combination of the different theme images alone creates impressive and therefore remarkable overall images (stories).

Furthermore, you no longer need to pay attention to the order of your card images on the positions in the image design! To take advantage of both these advantages - exercise provided - the memory of playing cards considerably.

The MLS / method occupies each playing card with three very different subject images, all of which are based in some way on the already known playing card images or topic areas (pages 130 to 133). The topics are:

M = Mankind - L = Lunch - S = Sport

➢ The first thing I chose to be the **M**ankind being is to activate pictorial thinking in your imagination.

➢ I chose the topic of **L**unch to activate as many senses as possible in your imagination, such as smelling, tasting, feeling, and so on.

➢ Last time, I chose **S**ports as a theme to bring movement and action into the previous pictures.

Example Queen of Diamonds:
With this playing card you have already saved the first card image (Mankind/human = castle damsel). The favorite dish or Lunch of the Queen of diamonds is pizza and the sport of the pretty lady is the pole vault.

M = castle damsel - **L** = pizza - **S** = pole vault

Example King of hearts:
Also with this playing card you have already saved the first card image (Man = Groom). The favorite dish of the Heart king is the suckling pig and the sport of the well-dressed gentleman is the shot-put.

M = Groom - **L** = Suckling pig - **S** = Shot put

Example Nine of clubs:
Here, too, you have already saved the first playing card image (mankind = bishop or bishop's staff). The bishop's lunch is kale and the sport of the churchman is sledding.

M = Bishop - **L** = Kale - **S** = Sledding

Again, it is very important that you get the extra
Imagine card images as imaginatively as possible!
Please also refer to pages 130 to 133.

In the MLS / method, the playing card images are distributed as usual to the positions of your lists. However, the playing card image always depends on whether the card is drawn first, second or third!

Order - MLS: 1. = Mankind 2. = Lunch 3. = Sport

Assuming that you want to remember the playing card combination 1. Diamond queen, 2. Heart King and 3. Club nine on the body list position 1, this results in the following overall picture on your foot:

➢ **M** = 1. card = Mankind, card image of Diamond queen = Damsel

➢ **L** = 2. Card = Lunch, card image of the Heart king = Suckling pig

➢ **S** = 3. Card = Sport, card image of the club Nine = Sledding

Her overall picture gives the combination: Damsel, suckling pig and sledding. Perhaps you imagine a sled damsel with a suckling pig between the teeth on your foot.
Or a suckling pig that has run over a damsel with his sled. You could also imagine a damsel passing a suckling pig with a sled.

If you want to remember later in which order the cards have fallen, simply sort them on your foot in the order MLS.

The nice thing is that these pictures are created by their crazy and strange combinations almost by itself! Nevertheless, the likelihood of confusion - even with very similar card combinations - equal to zero. Look for yourself:

Playing card combination: Club nine, Diamond queen and Heart king:

➢ M = 1. Card = Mankind, card image of Club nine = Bishop

➢ L = 2. Card = Lunch, card image of Diamond queen = Pizza

➢ S = 3. Card = Sport, card image of the Heart king = Shot put

Their overall picture is the combination: bishop, pizza and shot put. Imagine on position 2 of your body list, a bishop who is putting on a shotgun with a pizza.

Or a pizza, which is topped with chocolate Santas and Mozart balls.

You could also imagine a big bullet on which our Pope sits and eats an original Roman pizza.

Here is another variant:

Card combination: King of hearts, Nine of clubs and Queen of diamonds

➢ M = 1. Card = Mankind, Card image of the Heart king = Groom

➢ L = 2. Card = Lunch, Card image of the club 9 = Kale

➢ S = 3. Card = Sport, Card image of Diamond queen = Pole vault

To do this, you could imagine a groom on your thigh throwing a large bowl of kale over a high-jump lattice, etc.

In summary: The map picture of the respective map always depends on whether the map was drawn first (M), second (L) or third (S)! The order of images for your fantasy image does not matter, because you can easily sort them back by my MLS / Method anytime.

MLS at skat

The method can be applied to skat, even slightly modified. They assign a fixed theme ("mankind", "lunch" or "sport") to each player on the triple table (including himself) for the entire course of the game. However, the order of the playing cards or the pictures should be fixed here so that the individual stitches can be reconstructed.

Then, using this method, you can later tell not only which cards have already fallen, but also which player has placed a specific card.
In turn, you can draw valuable conclusions for the final. So, if you're thinking of searching for the King of Heart and finding it on your list as a "groom," it can only come from the player you've assigned the subject to "Mankind." However, you would need a fourth topic for the quad (see "Bridge").

If you play bridge

The same (see MLS at Skat) applies to other card game types.
For example, if you want to play bridge and place four cards in each position, just add another theme image.
Extend the Michael Lutz system with the animals mentioned on page 69.

MLS-A = Mankind, Lunch, Sport and Animal

It's not as complicated as it first seems, and it greatly speeds up the memory of playing card notes. It requires practice.
Always remember, therefore, that all the exercises in this book will have a very positive effect on your entire mindset.
And your brain will reward you with a much higher efficiency in quite different areas!

Michael Lutz System - Diamonds

Seven of diamonds = battle ax		Own pictures
Mankind	= Lumberjack	
Lunch	= Meatloaf	
Sports	= Cross-country skiing	
Eight of diamonds = Yoke		
Mankind	= Prisoner	
Lunch	= Bread	
Sports	= Weightlifting	
Nine of diamonds = Flag		
Mankind	= Standard bearer	
Lunch	= Pretzel	
Sports	= Curling	
Ten of diamonds = Lance		
Mankind	= Bushman	
Lunch	= Coconuts	
Sports	= Spear throwing	
Jack of diamonds = Squire		
Mankind	= Squire	
Lunch	= Red wine	
Sports	= Horseshoe aimed	
Queen of diamonds = Castle damsel		
Mankind	= Castle damsel	
Lunch	= Pizza	
Sports	= Pole vault	
Seven of diamonds = Knight		
Mankind	= Knight	
Lunch	= Trout	
Sports	= Fencing	
Ace of diamonds = Knight shield		
Mankind	= Gladiator	
Lunch	= Grapes	
Sports	= Chariot races	

Michael Lutz System – Hearts

Seven of hearts = Cloverleaf		Own pictures
Mankind	= Senner (meadow farmer)	
Lunch	= Cheese (fondue)	
Sports	= Golf	
Eight of hearts = Wedding ring		
Mankind	= Gold digger	
Lunch	= Steak	
Sports	= Rodeo	
Nine of hearts = Bridal bouquet		
Mankind	= Gardener	
Lunch	= Pumpkin	
Sports	= Lawn mower running	
Ten of hearts = Bed		
Mankind	= Patient	
Lunch	= Pills cocktail (drip)	
Sports	= Mattress jumping	
Jack of hearts = Baby		
Mankind	= Baby	
Lunch	= Vial	
Sports	= Pacifier wide throw	
Queen of hearts = Bride		
Mankind	= Bride	
Lunch	= White cabbage (	
Sports	= Dancing	
King of hearts = Groom		
Mankind	= Groom	
Lunch	= Suckling pig	
Sports	= Shot put	
Ace of hearts = Wedding carriage		
Mankind	= Coachman	
Lunch	= (Horse) apples	
Sports	= Show jumping	

Michael Lutz System – Spades

Seven of spades = Earth hoe		Own pictures
Mankind	= Eskimo	
Lunch	= Walrus bacon	
Sports	= Ice hockey	
Eight of spades = Concrete pipe		
Mankind	= Astronaut	
Lunch	= Venus shells	
Sports	= Tower jump	
Nine of spades = Wheelbarrow		
Mankind	= Rickshaw driver)	
Lunch	= Rice dishes	
Sports	= Barre gymnastics	
Ten of spades = Bulldozer		
Mankind	= Racer	
Lunch	= Champagne	
Sports	= Formula 1	
Jack of spades = Sandbox		
Mankind	= Bedouin	
Lunch	= Figs	
Sports	= Camel race	
Queen of spades = Alice Schwarzer		
Mankind	= Alice Schwarzer	
Lunch	= Lemon chicken à la Alice	
Sports	= Boxes	
King of spades = Helmet		
Mankind	= Construction worker	
Lunch	= Goat sausage	
Sports	= Bowling	
Ace of spades = Astute saw		
Mankind	= Tarzan	
Lunch	= Bananas	
Sports	= Archery	

Michael Lutz System – Clubs

Seven of clubs = Coffin		Own pictures
Mankind	= Vampire	
Lunch	= Blood sausage	
Sports	= Paragliding	
Eight of clubs = Tombstone		
Mankind	= Stone Age man	
Lunch	= Mammoth roast	
Sports	= Club throw	
Nine of clubs = Crosier		
Mankind	= Bishop	
Lunch	= Kale	
Sports	= Sledding	
Ten of clubs = Bible		
Mankind	= Monk	
Lunch	= Chocolate	
Sports	= Water skiing	
Jack of clubs = Natavity scene		
Mankind	= Virgin Mary	
Lunch	= Blueberries	
Sports	= Badminton	
Queen of clubs = Widow		
Mankind	= Widow	
Lunch	= Black tagliatelle	
Sports	= Sailing	
King of clubs = Icon		
Mankind	= Painter	
Lunch	= Spread cheese	
Sports	= Tug of war	
Ace of clubs of clubs = Vulture		
Mankind	= Pilot	
Lunch	= Vulture eggs	
Sports	= Aerobatics	

Using the example of Mr. Wolfgang Berghammer and the shopping list, I have already reminded you that with this memory technique you can not only memorize playing cards.
How you easily and permanently remember numbers, I would like to illustrate in the following chapter.

Remember numbers quickly and permanently

I would like to ask you to take a brief look at the numbers below.

Now try to estimate how long it will take you to memorize the numbers so that you can play them out of your memory in the correct order the next day.

| 97012018910206159117121601929413089904119519051410 |

Most likely, at the sight of this number, you will now have had something of the feeling you felt at the beginning of this book, when I asked you to remember as many of the cards I had counted as possible.

Maybe you will not even have tried to estimate how long you would need for this. You can memorize the above-mentioned 50-digit number with the memory technique that you have already learned in this self-study, in a few minutes permanently, although you are - as regards memory techniques - still in the beginning and are relatively inexperienced.
All you have to do is change your card-memory technique a bit and use your previous knowledge in the form of your lists with the corresponding positions.

For this purpose, I will now also solve the mystery why we have each of the 10 lists always occupied with 10 positions.
Part of the technique that you used to remember playing cards is now also used for the numbers! If you believe that you need to produce number images or even topic areas for your abstract numbers, I can reassure you!

Your number images have already been saved, in the form of the positions on your lists!

With your 10 lists and the associated positions you have already anchored 100 pictures for 100 numbers in your memory.

For example, for the number 11, you have football with its substitute pictures, such as a football goal, football field, etc. What do you see in the
number 91 in your mind's eye? Right, your foot. And so on.

If you consider all digits of the 50-digit number as 2-digits (the Ape, for
example, stands for the 01, the bear for 02, etc.), you only need to remember 25 images to save this number safely,

A 50-digit number in a few minutes

You can do the same with your already existing number images as with
your map images.

Simply distribute them in the form of little stories on the individual positions of your lists.

To give you an example, we will occupy the first five positions of your
zoolist with the 50-digit number. To do this, divide the number into five
blocks of ten (separated by hyphens).

9701201891 – 0206159117 – 1216019294 – 1308990411 – 9519051410

Since we consider all numbers and the associated number images as 2-
digit, each block of ten consists of five numbers (separated by commas).

➢	Ape/Monkey =	97, 01, 20, 18, 91
➢	Bear =	02, 06, 15, 91, 17
➢	Chameleon =	12, 16, 01, 92, 94
➢	Dolphin =	13, 08, 99, 04, 11
➢	Elephant =	95, 19, 05, 14, 10

Now imagine that you enter the first five floors of your »zoo« (zoo list)
one after the other. First, you come to the apes house and suddenly feel
a heavy blow on your shoulder (97), because one of the Apes (01)
jumped on your shoulder. The Ape on your shoulder now puts a huge
bottle of beer (20) on his mouth to drink from it. At that moment, a soldier
(18) runs up to you, takes away the bottle of beer from the Ape on your
shoulder and painfully hits your left foot with the bottle (91).

Please try to experience these and the four following little stories after the
reading again in your mind's eye.

> Zoo list position 1 = Ape:
>
> Shoulder 97, Ape 01, Beer 20, Soldier 18 and Foot 91
>
> 97– 01– 20 –18 – 91

On the 2nd floor of your zoo list you will see a large bear (02) riding a hippopotamus (06). Since this hippopotamus looks exhausted, give the poor animal a big cake (15) to eat. The hippopotamus grabs the cake with its big mouth so greedily that it steps on the big toe of your right foot (91), and immediately a young girl with blonde hair (17) comes rushing over to help you.

> Zoo list Position 2 = Bear:
>
> Bear 02, Hippopotamus 06, Cake 15, Foot 91 and Girl 17
>
> 02 – 06 –15 – 91–17

As you step onto the chameleon floor of your zoo list, you see a cowboy (12) on a motorcycle (16) swinging a lasso after a ape (01) because it had annoyed him beforehand. When the cowboy has caught the ape, he puts it over his knee (92) and spanks his butt with his lasso (94).

> Zoo list Position 3 = Chameleon:
>
> Cowboy 12, Motorcycle 16, Ape 01, Knees 92 and Buttocks 94
>
> 12 –16 – 01– 92 – 94

On the 4th floor you can see how a chimney sweep (13) competes with a dog (08) in the pool that is actually intended for the dolphins. The dog wins the swimming competition against the chimney sweep and hits the edge of the pool with his sensitive dog nose (99). At this very moment the dog turns into a dolphin (04), which is balancing an oversized football (11) on its pointed snout.

> Zoo list Position 4 = Dolphin:
>
> Chimney sweep 13, Dog 08, Nose 99, Dolphin 04 and Football 11
>
> 13 – 08 – 99 – 04 –11

When you are about to enter the 5th floor of the Elephants, it seems like the door is stuck. You try to batter-ram open the door with your hip, which you succeed in doing. When the door pops open, many firework rockets (19) come whistling towards you, which the elephants (05) fire at you from their trunks. At this very moment, a small, two-seat, open airplane (14), whose pilot is a Jeti (10), lands behind you and flies you out of the danger zone.

Zoo list Position 5 = Elephant:
Hip 95, Fireworks 19, Elephant 05, Airplane 14, and Jeti 10
95 –19 – 05 –14 –10

Please also note the summary on page 138..

Numbers in a different way

Position 1, Ape:

➢	Shoulder	= 97
➢	Ape	= 01
➢	Beer	= 20
➢	Soldier	= 18
➢	Feet	= 91

Position 2, Bear:

➢	Bear	= 02
➢	Hippopotamus	= 06
➢	Cake	= 15
➢	Feet	= 91
➢	Girl	= 17

Position 3, Chameleon:

➢	Cowboy	= 12
➢	Motorcycle	= 16
➢	Ape	= 01
➢	Knee	= 92
➢	Buttocks	= 94

Position 4, Dolphin:

➢	Chimney sweep	= 13
➢	Dog	= 08
➢	Nose	= 99
➢	Dolphin	= 04
➢	Footbal	= 11

Position 5, Elephant:

➢	Hip	= 95
➢	Firework rocket	= 19
➢	Elephant	= 05
➢	Airplane	= 14
➢	Jeti	= 10

It's really a completely different way of dealing with numbers, isn't it? I am sure that in the future you will not forget the PIN number of your check card, etc. so quickly.

For example, try to remember what the 30th digit, the 18th digit, and so on was. You can even do that because you have structured the 50-digit number in your memory accordingly.

This is just one of many examples of how you can expand and expand your current knowledge of mnemonics with very little effort.

Meaning and resolution of the 10 stories
(The playing card list structured with key frames)

Playing card	Follow Position	List card image
1. Ten of spades	Foot	Bulldozer
2. Queen of diamonds	Foot	Castle damsel
3. Nine of hearts	Foot	Bridal bouquet
4. Jack of hearts	Knee	Baby
5. Seven of spades	Knee	Earth hoe
6. King of spades	Knee	Helmet
7. Jack of clubs	Thigh	Natavity scene
8. Nine of spades	Thigh	Wheelbarrow
9. Ten of clubs	Thigh	Bible
10. King of diamonds	Butthocks	Knight
11. Ten of diamonds	Butthocks	Lance
12. Queen of clubs	Butthocks	Widow
13. Seven of hearts	Hip	Cloverleaf
14. King of clubs	Hip	Icon
15. Eight of hearts	Hip	Weddingring
16. Eight of clubs	Chest	Tombstone
17. Ace of clubs	Chest	Vulture
18. Ace of spades	Chest	Astute saw
19. Jack of spades	Shoulder	Sandbox
20. Queen of hearts	Shoulder	Bride
21. Eight of spades	Shoulder	Concrete pipe
22. Eight of diamonds	Neck	Yoke
23. King of hearts	Neck	Bridegroom
24. Seven of diamonds	Neck	Battle ax
25. Ace of hearts	Nose	Wedding carriage
26. Jack of diamonds	Nose	Squire
27. Queen of spades	Nose	Alice Schwarzer
28. Ten of hearts	Hair	Bed
29. Seven of clubs	Hair	Coffin
30. Nine of diamonds	Hair	Flagg

Summary of all playing card values and card images
(Subject areas sorted by card color and Subject areas)
Diamonds: Knight/Middle Ages - **Hearts:** Love/marriage/happines
Spades: Construction site/work - **Clubs:** Church/death/funeral

Playing card	Card images	Reason
Seven of diamonds	Battle axe	The shape of the 7 resembles a battle axe.
Eight of diamonds	Yoke	The holes for the arms resemble a horizontal figure 8.
Nine of diamonds	Flag	The shape of the 9 is reminiscent of one Flag.
Ten of diamonds	Lance	The 1 resembles a lance.
Jack of diamonds	Squire	The knight's squire was mostly small and fat.
Queen of diamonds	Castle damsel	There was about the damsel Knight tournaments.
King of diamonds	Knight	The knight served the king.
Ace of diamonds *	A knight's shield	Playing card as a shield made of sheet metal and with a handle.
Seven of hearts	Cloverleaf	7 and cloverleaf represent luck.
Eight of hearts	Wedding rings	The 8 looks like 2 rings on top of each other.
Nine of hearts	Bridal bouquet	The shape of the number resembles a bouquet of flowers.
Ten of hearts	Bed	1 is the bed, 0 is the blanket, rotated by 90 degrees.
Jack of hearts	Baby	A baby is the result of the love.
Queen of hearts	Bride	The bride is (hopefully) the lady of the heart.
King of hearts	Bridegroom	The Lord of the Heart is natural the Bridegroom.

Ace of hearts	Wedding carriage	The shape of the word – ace – resembles a carriage.
Seven of spades	Earth hoe	The 7 is shaped like a hoe.
Eight of spades	Concrete pipe	The 8 looks like two pipes on top of each other.
Nine of spades	Wheelbarrow	The 9, rotated 90 degrees, is reminiscent of a wheelbarrow.
Ten of spades	Bulldozer	The 1 is a shovel, 0 is the drive wheel or vehicle.
Jack of spades	Sandbox	A child builds a sand castle in it.
Queen of spades	Alice Schwarzer	She would also work on a construction site.
King of spades	Helmet	The king wears a construction helmet instead of a crown.
Ace of spades	Astute saw	The word says it all: as-t-saw.
Seven of clubs	Coffin	The 7 is equal to a half opened coffin.
Eight of clubs	Tombstone	The 8 is above the 7 of clubs, the coffin.
Nine of clubs *	Bishop's crook	The 9 resembles a bishop's crook.
Ten of clubs	Bible	It contains the 10 commandments.
Jack of clubs	Natavity scene	The son of God, his boy, lies in the manger.
Queen of clubs	Widow	The widow wears all black.
King of clubs	Icon	It shows the image of God highest king.
Ace of clubs	Vulture	He eats carrion and is a symbol of death.

*The two cards marked with an asterisk were not included in the 10 stories on our body list!

Seven of diamonds = Battle axe

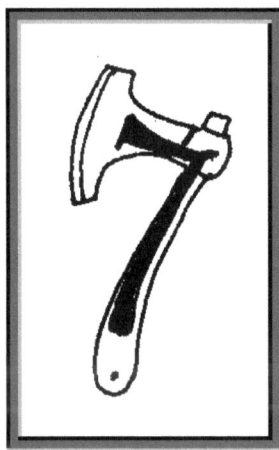

Subject area: Knights/Middle Ages

Reason for the picture: The shape of the number 7 resembles a battle axe. Possible replacement images: hatchet, ax and all types of edged weapons such as halberd, sword, executioner's ax, knife, etc.

Seven of diamonds

Subject area: _____

Replacement images: _____

Eight of diamonds = Yoke

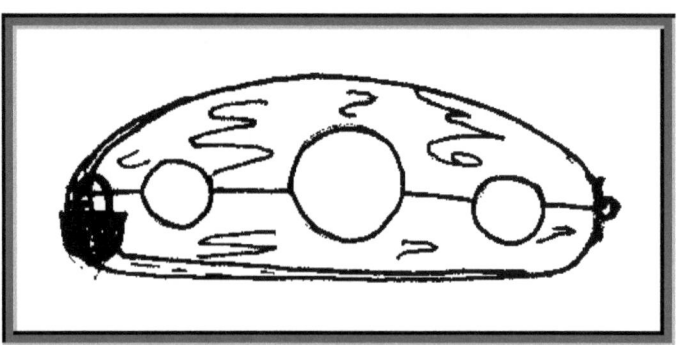

Eight of diamonds

Subject area: _____

Replacement images: _____

Nine of diamonds = Flag

Subject area: Knights/Middle Ages
Reason for the picture: The shape of the number 9 is reminiscent of a flag. Possible replacement images: pennant, flag, towel, bath towel, etc. Caution: Do not use any towels or blankets that have anything to do with a bed! They could be confused with the 10 of hearts (bed)!

Nine of diamonds

Subject area: _____

Replacement images: _____

Ten of diamonds = Lance

Subject area: Knights/Middle Ages
Reason for the picture: The shape of the lance, with a small pennant.
Possible replacement images: Anything that has to do with needles, such as: E.g. sewing needle, knitting needle, safety pin etc.
Caution: If possible, do not use other weapons as they could be confused with the Karo 7 (battle axe)!

Ten of diamonds

Subject area: _____

Replacement images: _____

Jack of diamonds = Squire

Subject area: Knights/Middle Ages

Reason for the picture: The squire is the weapon bearer and henchman of the knight (king of diamonds); he is also below him in card value.
Possible replacement images: Anything related to Don Quixote or Sancho Panza, such as: E.g. windmills, giants etc.

Jack of diamonds

Subject area: _____

Replacement images: _____

Queen of diamonds = Castle damsel

Subject area: Knights/Middle Ages
Reason for the picture: During tournaments held by the damsels, the knights regularly dented their pewter hats.
Possible replacement images: Anything that has to do with grace and beautiful women, such as ballet.

Queen of diamonds

Subject area: _____

Replacement images: _____

148

King of diamonds = Ritter

Subject area: Knights/Middle Ages
Reason for the picture: The knight served the king. Possible replacement images: Anything related to a castle, such as: E.g. drawbridge, moat, tower pinnacle, etc. Attention: If possible, do not take weapons as they could be confused with other card images! Like for example: 7 diamonds (battle axe) or 10 diamonds (lance)!

King of diamonds

Subject area: _____

Replacement images: _____

Ace of diamonds = A knight's shield

Ace of diamonds

Subject area: _____

Replacement images: _____

Seven of hearts = Cloverleaf

Subject area: Love/marriage/happiness
Reason for the picture: The number 7 and the clover symbolize luck.
Possible replacement images: All kinds of lucky symbols, such as pigs, lucky pennies, rabbit feet, etc.
Caution: Do not take other types of flowers, they could come into contact with the Heart 9 (bridal bouquet) can be confused!

Seven of hearts

Subject area: _____

Replacement images:_____

Eight of hearts = Wedding rings

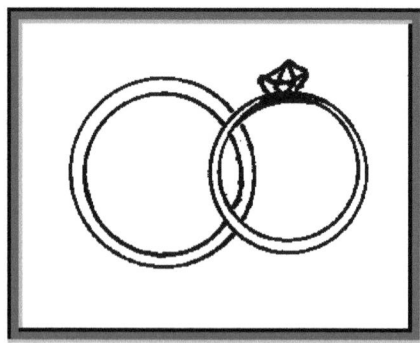

Subject area: Love/marriage/happiness
Reason for the picture: The number 8 has the shape of two rings placed one on top of the other.Possible replacement images: signet ring, diamond ring, bangles and all other types of jewelry.

Eight of hearts

Subject area: _____

Replacement images: _____

Nine of hearts = Bridal bouquet

Subject area: Love/marriage/happiness
Reason for the picture: The shape of the number 9. At the top of the head of the 9 are the flowers, at the bottom are the flower stems that serve as handles.
Possible replacement images: All types of flowers or anything that has to do with plants, such as sunflowers, roses, florist, greenhouse, etc.

Nine of hearts

Subject area: _____

Replacement images: _____

Ten of hearts = Bed

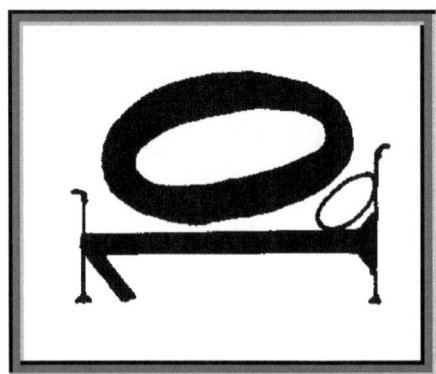

Subject area: Love/marriage/happiness
Reason for the picture: Why I associate a bed with love, of all things, I would like to leave to your own imagination.
Possible replacement images: All types of beds, such as canopy beds, bunk beds, water beds, camp beds, but also air mattresses, hammocks, etc.

Ten of hearts

Subject area: _____

Replacement images: _____

Jack of hearts = Baby

Jack of hearts

Subject area: _____

Replacement images: _____

Queen of hearts = Bride

Subject area: Love/marriage/happiness
Reason for the picture: You only marry the lady of your heart. Possible replacement images: Princess, queen, any woman who is dressed conspicuously, including a beggar or a homeless woman.

Queen of hearts

Subject area: _____

Replacement images: _____

King of hearts = Bridegroom

Subject area: Love/marriage/happiness
Reason for the picture: The lady of hearts marries the king of her heart.
Possible replacement images due to the tailcoat: conductor, hotel porter,
head waiter, penguin etc.

King of hearts

Subject area: _____

Replacement images: _____

Ace of hearts = Wedding carriage

Subject area: Love/marriage/happiness
Reason for the picture: The shape of the capital "A" could be thought of as a carriage and the shape of the small "S" as the horse.
Possible replacement images: All types of transportation that are pulled by horses or other animals.
Caution: Do not use implements (for example: plow) that are pulled by animals; they could be confused with the topic of spades (construction site/work)!

Ace of hearts

Subject area: _____

Replacement images: _____

Seven of spades = Earth hoe

Subject Area: Construction site/work

Reason for the picture: When placed upright, the hoe has the shape of a 7. Possible replacement images: sledgehammer, shovel, spade and anything else that has to do with earthwork or gardening.

Caution: Do not use any work tools (for example a plow) that are pulled by animals, as they could be confused with the heart theme (wedding carriage)!

Seven of spades

Subject area: _____

Replacement images: _____

Eight of spades = Concrete pipe

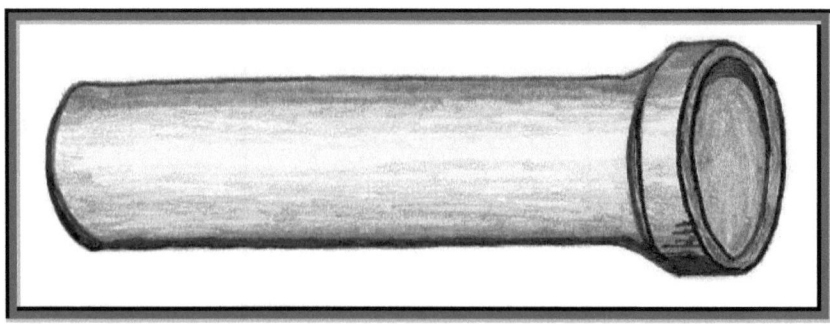

Eight of spades

Subject area: _____

Replacement images: _____

Nine of spades = Wheelbarrow

Nine of spades

Subject area: _____

Replacement images: _____

Ten of spades = Bulldozer

Subject Area: Construction site/work
Reason for the picture: The number 1 represents the shovel, the number 0 the drive wheel or the vehicle itself.
Possible replacement images: snow plow, recovery vehicle, excavator, semi-trailer, tipper, tractor, combine harvester, crane truck and all other vehicles that are used as commercial vehicles.

Ten of spades

Subject area: _____

Replacement images: _____

Jack of spades = Sandbox

Subject Area: Construction site/work
Reason for the picture: A child (boy) could build a sandcastle in the sandpit.
Possible replacement images: anything that has to do with sand, such as: E.g. beach, sand pile, desert, dune, sandstorm etc.

Jack of spades

Subject area: _____

Replacement images: _____

Queen of spades = Alice Schwarzer

Queen of spades

Subject area: _____

Replacement images: _____

King of spades = Helmet

Subject Area: Construction site/work
Reason for the picture: The king has run out of money, so he has to build his own castle. To do this, he exchanges his crown for a construction helmet.
Possible replacement images: steel helmet, turtle, bunker, umbrella and of course all kinds of hats.

King of spades

Subject area: _____

Replacement images: _____

Ace of spades = Astute saw

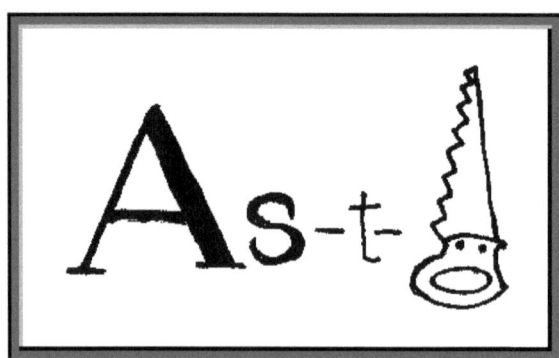

Subject Area: Construction site/work

Reason for the picture:The word branch saw begins with "As" and the saw is reminiscent of the construction site/work theme.

Possible replacement images: hacksaw, steel saw, tree saw, chainsaw, sawdust, sawmill and everything else that is related to sawing.

Ace of spades

Subject area: _____

Replacement images: _____

Seven of clubs = Coffin

Subject Area: Church/Death/Funeral
Reason for the picture: A coffin sawn lengthwise without a lid looks like the number 7 from the front.Possible replacement images: box, cupboard, grave, grave lamp, grave bowl, urn, hole, cemetery chapel - because that's where the coffin is laid out - etc.

Seven of clubs 7

Subject area: _____

Replacement images: _____

Eight of clubs = Tombstone

Eight of clubs

Subject area: _____

Replacement images: _____

Nine of clubs = Bishop´s crook

Subject Area: Church/Death/Funeral
Reason for the picture: The number 9 resembles a bishop's crook.
Possible replacement images: bishop, pope, scepter, orb, crucifix, etc.

Nine of clubs

Subject area: _____

Replacement images: _____

Ten of clubs = Bible

Subject Area: Church/Death/Funeral
Reason for the picture: The Ten Commandments are in the Bible.
Possible replacement images: "Normal" books, sheets of paper, confetti, streamers and anything made entirely of paper.

Ten of clubs

Subject area: _____

Replacement images: _____

Jack of clubs = Natavity scene

Subject Area: Church/Death/Funeral

Reason for the picture:
The Son of God, his boy, lies in the nativity scene.
Possible replacement images: stable, Three Wise Men, stars, comets, etc. Caution: No images that have to do with infants, strollers, etc., as they could be confused with the Jack of Hearts (baby)!

Jack of clubs

Subject area: _____

Replacement images: _____

Queen of clubs = Widow

Subject Area: Church/Death/Funeral
The Widow was the 12th key image in the 4th position (buttocks).
Reason for the picture: The widow is dressed entirely in black (clubs) and is therefore a black lady.
Possible replacement images: black veil, mourning ribbon, black gloves or handkerchiefs, etc.

Queen of clubs

Subject area: _____

Replacement images: _____

King of clubs = Icon

Subject Area: Church/Death/Funeral

Reason for the picture:An icon shows the image of God, the supreme king.Possible replacement images: images of saints of all kinds, monastery work, religious carvings such as figures of saints, etc.

Caution: Do not take any ecclesiastical items made of metal, as they could be confused with the Nine of Clubs!

King of clubs

Subject area: _____

Replacement images: _____

Ace of clubs = Vulture

Subject Area: Church/Death/Funeral
Reason for the picture:
The vulture eats carrion and is a symbol of death.
Possible replacement images: eagle, cormorant, desert, raw, rotten meat, dead animals, etc.

Ace of clubs

Subject area: _____

Replacement images: _____

Before you start the second chapter

Anything you want to learn will get better with practice and will inevitably become easier for you. The more often you work with your lists and card images, the faster these processes will run.

This self-study course has already been an excellent and efficient memory training for you. Regular use of these special memory techniques is an excellent way to actively take action for yourself as a preventative measure against dementia.

Maintain your newly acquired knowledge, because if you neglect it, you will lose it again, just as you can lose a foreign language or even your native language after many years abroad if you do not use it at least occasionally.

Chapter 2

Hand on the heart ... better still on the brain

...did you skip the first chapter?

In the second chapter we will largely limit ourselves to the practical applications of memory techniques for Black Jack (matrix tables) and brain-friendly card counting.

If you skipped the first chapter, I assume that you are more interested in Black Jack than in the connections between the brain and memory.

However, since this deprives you of crucial background knowledge, it inevitably means that some techniques will seem a bit crazy or even strange to you. Therefore a request to you:

> Try to implement the exercises "1 to 1" if possible.
> **It works!**

The combination of basic and card counting strategy is what makes Black Jack the only casino game that gives the player a real advantage over the bank.

In this chapter you will find memory strategies on the topics:

>> When you should double your bet

>> Which card combinations you can and should split up

>> When to buy or not buy in a hard or soft hand

>> How to count cards successfully and practically

I will show you in the truest sense of the word with the help of the memory techniques developed specifically for the game of Black Jack!

The following information and game rules are limited to European standards. All tables and recommendations are without guarantee and are primarily intended to serve as an example of how you can easily and, above all, memorize complicated facts, number combinations, etc. relating to the game of Black Jack in a brain-friendly manner.

Basic rules Black Jack

Black Jack's basic structure is comparable to "17 and 4".
In the game of Black Jack, each card represents a specific point value.
The aim of the game is to get a better hand than the bank.

Card point values:

Aces count (at the player's choice) either 11 points or 1 point.
Pictures (Jacks, Queens and Kings) count 10 points.
All other cards count the printed point value.
Color values such as diamonds, hearts etc. have no meaning.

Game and rules:

Each player receives two cards from the dealer/croupier - dealt face up.
The bank receives one card face up and one face down.
After dealing cards, you decide whether you want to buy more cards (hit)
or not (stand).
If the last player at the table no longer wants to buy a card, the
dealer/croupier draws additional cards according to the following rules:
If he has a point value of 16 or less, he must buy another card. From 17
points onwards he is no longer allowed to take cards. In contrast to the
dealer/croupier, the player is allowed to buy additional cards or fold with
each score.

Win and loss:

The player always loses if the sum of his card points is higher than 21
(bust).
If the player did not bust, he always won when the bank busted, or:
If he has more card points than the bank, or:
If he has Black Jack (21 points with 2 cards) and the bank does not have
Black Jack.
If the player has the same number of points as the dealer/croupier, it is
considered a draw (push) and no one wins or loses.

Insurance/protection:

If the bank's first face-up card is an ace, you have the option to insure yourself against a black jack from the bank (insurance).
To do this, you bet an amount equal to half of your stake
Insurance line of the gaming table.
If the bank then has a Black Jack, you will receive double your insurance amount. If the bank doesn't have Black Jack, your insurance bet is lost.

Basic strategy

In order to play Black Jack as successfully and efficiently as possible, you not only have to master the rules of the game, but you also have to have numerous card combinations - in the form of tables - safely stored in your "upper room".
The most important tables are:

1. Double:
This table shows you which card combinations can - and should - double your stake.

2. Splitting:
This table shows you which card combinations you can - and should - split two identical cards.

3. Buy – Hard hand:
This table shows you which card combinations you should buy or not buy in a hard hand.

4. Buy – Soft hand (Ace still counts 11 points):
This table shows you which card combinations you should buy or not buy in a soft hand.

> A detailed explanation of the aforementioned basics
> can be found in the respective table graphics!

All tables offer you extremely valuable information and advice on when, how and what you should do with which card combination in order to play Black Jack as efficiently as possible.
At least in theory!
Unfortunately, such tables are very difficult to remember and usually cannot be recalled from memory quickly enough during a game, as our brain only processes them as digital and therefore abstract (non-objective) information.
As shown in the first chapter, digital information such as numbers, formulas and the aforementioned basics can be memorized or accessed much better and faster if we visualize them and organize them in a brain-friendly way (structure)!

That means:

In practical use, the first thing you have to do is memorize a fixed list of mentally visualized numbers. The following "number pictures list" is particularly easy to remember in its order because I give you the corresponding associations (links). This list will be even more memorable if you also mentally create your own visual associations.

> Please remember this list as best you can.
> You will also need this list later when counting cards!

The number picture list

Number pictures	Associations
1. Tree	The tree trunk looks like a Roman 1
2. Light switch	Switch positions, on – off, light – dark
3. Stool	Usually has 3 chair legs
4. Car	Has 4 wheels, 4 seats, 4 gears etc.
5. Hand	The hand has 5 fingers
6. Dice	6 numbers, 6 dice sides
7. Dwarf	Snow White and the 7 Dwarfs
8. Roller coaster	Often drives in the form of an 8 - "eight"
9. Cat	They say she has 9 lives
10. Bible	Because of the 10 Commandments
11. Football	Number of players,"The Soccer eleven""
12. Ghost	The time at 12 o'clock, the witching hour
13. Elevator	There is no 13th floor in the hotel
14. Heart	February 14th is Valentine's Day
15. Knight	15th century, the Middle Ages
16. Teenager	The song: sweet sixteen, 16 years
17. Card game	"17 and 4" the card game
18. Closing time	The time; home from work
19. Dinner	The time; is dinner at 7 p.m
20. TV news	The news starts at 8 p.m

Table structure

After you have successfully visualized 20 numbers, illustrate the framework structure of the following 4 tables.

Please try to imagine these and subsequent pictures or stories as clearly, colorfully and crazy as possible!

The better and more memorable you mentally (mentally) produce your pictures and stories, the better and faster they can be re-produced (remembered) later!

Imagine the 4 tables as 4 car garages, which - apart from the gate - all look the same on the outside and are arranged next to each other from left to right.

Doubling the stake:
The first garage has an outdated wooden garage door consisting of two panels. She has a double door.

Splitting/dividing two identical cards:
The second garage is a glass garage door. Because the glass gate is always stuck, hit it with a heavy sledgehammer every time so that it breaks into a thousand splinters.

Hard hand - special card combinations:
Garage door number 3 is very valuable because it is covered in diamonds.Diamond is the hardest material on earth.

Soft hand - special card combinations:
The fourth and final garage does not have a garage door! Instead, there is an oversized soft ice cream machine in the driveway that you have to laboriously push aside every time you want to get in.

Please try to bring these images to life in your mind's eye for at least 5 minutes and "visit" these places mentally.

Double your bet

If your first two cards total 9, 10 or 11 points, you should double your bet for certain card combinations - depending on the bank's cards.
Note: You will then only receive one more card.

The table below shows which card combinations you should double down on (X) and when not (-)

Your points	Bank card									
	2	3	4	5	6	7	8	9	10	Ace
9	-	x	x	x	x	-	-	-	-	-
10	x	x	x	x	x	x	x	x	-	-
11	x	x	x	x	x	x	x	x	-	-

Example of the schematic representation of the table:
Your total card points/values > 9 <

Your points	Bank card									
	2	3	4	5	6	7	8	9	10	Ace
9	-	X	X	X	X	-	-	-	-	-
10	x	x	x	x	x	x	x	x	-	-
11	x	x	x	x	x	x	x	x	-	-

For example, if your first two cards are a 7 and a 2 - for a total of 9 points - and the bank has a 3 (or 4, 5 and 6), you should double your bet.

For example, if your first two cards are a 5 and a 4 (which adds up to 9 points) and the bank has a 2 (or 7, 8, 9, 10, and Ace), you should not double your bet.

How to memorize these and subsequent tables quickly, easily and safely

First, something fundamental:

For all tables, only remember the positive (X) combinations!
Positive (X) combinations mean you should take action.
In this case - **double your bet!**

Negative (-) combinations mean that you remain passive (even when remembering).
In this case - **do not double your bet!**

For the first position of our table, the 9 (total score of your first two cards), you only take into account the 4 positive combinations (X) 3, 4, 5 and 6!

With a few exceptions, you only need to memorize - even with the other tables - the front and back positives of the card combinations (in this case the 3 and 6).
Because:
The points between 3 and 6 (4 and 5) are also positive!

Please only continue reading once you have understood all previous statements and explanations 100% and have at least memorized the list of numbers to some extent!

As mentioned at the beginning, we remember digital information such as numbers and tables better if we visualize them and organize them in a brain-friendly way. For exactly this purpose, you have memorized the tree list and the four garages, which you can now put to practical use for the first time.

Double - remember the total points

For example, if you want to remember which total points of your first two cards are suitable for doubling, just imagine the following situation:

The first garage has an outdated wooden garage door consisting of two rotten doors. It has, so to speak, a double door (doubling).
You go to your first garage and open the two (**double**) wooden double doors - with a loud grinding and squeaking noise.
On the left wall of the garage you see a loudly purring (**Cat (9)**, on the head wall a large **Bible (10)** decorated with gold and precious stones and on the right wall of the garage, imagine a soccer ball (11, soccer ball) that you have nailed there!

> Please try the "furnishings" of your first
> Imagine the garage as vividly and movingly as possible!

The left wall, head wall and right wall of your garage represent the spatial order or sequence - always from left to right (clockwise) - of your table.

1 = Left wall, **9 = Cat**
2 = middle of headboard, **10 = Bible**
3 = Right wall, **11 = Football**

9 Cat, 10 Bible and 11 Football are the total scores of your first two cards, in the table below (double door garage).

Double door garage

Your points	Bank card									
	2	3	4	5	6	7	8	9	10	Ace
9 = Cat	-	x	x	x	x	-	-	-	-	-
10 = Bible	x	x	x	x	x	x	x	x	-	-
11 = Football	x	x	x	x	x	x	x	x	-	-

Double your bet: Your total card points > 9 <
(Total points = The first two cards)

Your points	Bank card									
	2	**3**	4	5	**6**	7	8	9	10	Ace
9 Cat	–	**X Stool**	X Car	X Hand	**X Dice**	–	–	–	–	–
10	x	x	x	x	x	x	x	x	-	-
11	x	x	x	x	x	x	x	x	-	-

Now imagine that on the left wall of the **double**-door garage the **cat** (9 = total number of points from your first two cards) would jump onto a **stool** (3 = front positive card value) and then roll a **dice** with a dice cup (6 = rear positive card value)!

As a reminder, the points between the bank's card values, 3 and 6 (4 and 5), are also **positive!** All you really need to remember is 9 = cat, 3 = stool and 6 = dice.

In one sentence:
If the total score of your first two cards is 9 points and the bank's face-up card is a 3, 4, 5 or 6, you should double your bet.

Double your bet: Your total card points > 10 <

Your points	Bank card									
	2	3	4	5	6	7	8	9	10	Ace
9	-	x	x	x	x	-	-	-	-	-
10 Bible	**X Light switch**	x	x	x	x	x	x	**X Cat**	-	-
11	x	x	x	x	x	x	x	x	-	-

On the head wall of your double-door garage is a valuable **Bible** decorated with gold fittings and precious stones (10 = total score of your first two cards).

The splendor of the Bible only really comes into its own when you turn on the **light switch** (2 = front positive card value) in the garage. Another light-sensitive **cat** (9 = rear positive card value) - which sits on this Bible - does not like the resulting bright shine of the Bible at all and therefore hisses at you angrily!

Recommendation: Stories and images that you think up yourself and decorate with your own imagination are more memorable than stories and images that are given to you from outside - for example the author.

Double your bet: Your total card points > 11 <

Your points	Bank card									
	2	3	4	5	6	7	8	9	10	Ace
9	-	x	x	x	x	-	-	-	-	-
10	x	x	x	x	x	x	x	x	-	-
11 Football	**X Light switch**	x	x	x	x	x	x	**X Cat**	-	-

On the right wall of your double-door garage hangs a strange **soccer ball** (11 = total number of points from your first two cards). An electronic **toggle switch** (light switch = front positive card value) is attached to this. Every time you press the toggle switch, the football briefly turns into a big roaring **lion** (cat 9 = rear positive card value)!

Surely you have noticed,
that I used an "electronic toggle switch" for the number image of 2 instead of a light switch and replaced the number image of 9, the cat, with a "big lion" (big cat).
Despite these apparent "mistakes," you don't run the risk of remembering the wrong number images. Because:
You're unlikely to confuse an electronic toggle switch with a cat or a lion with a light switch!
So let your imagination run wild when creating your own stories.

When you should double your stake Summary

Your points	Bank card									
	2	3	4	5	6	7	8	9	10	Ace
9 Cat Left wall	-	**Stool**	x	x	**Dice**	-	-	-	-	-
10 Bibel Head wall	**Light switch**	x	x	x	x	x	x	**Cat**	-	-
11 Football Right wall	**Light switch**	x	x	x	x	x	x	**Cat**	-	-

Gray background = Become positive/active and doublen

! Just remember the fields highlighted in gray!

White = Stay negative/passive, don't double down

Please summarize the stories and number pictures in your **double**-door garage one or more times mentally and with a lot of imagination.

Splitting – dividing the cards

If your first two cards have the same point value, you can split/divide your cards.
Here you double your original stake because you are now spreading your cards over two hands.
You can buy as many cards as you want for each hand, with one exception:
If you split two Aces, you only get one more card for each Ace.
An ace with a 10 or a picture is not considered blackjack in a split game, but counts as "only" 21 points.

Please see the table below
which card combinations you should split (X)
and when not (-)

Your cards	Bank card									
	2	3	4	5	6	7	8	9	10	Ace
2,2	-	-	x	x	x	x	-	-	-	-
3,3	-	-	x	x	x	x	-	-	-	-
4,4	-	-	-	-	-	-	-	-	-	-
5,5	-	-	-	-	-	-	-	-	-	-
6,6	-	x	x	x	x	-	-	-	-	-
7,7	x	x	x	x	x	x	-	-	-	-
8,8	x	x	x	x	x	x	x	x	-	-
9,9	x	x	x	x	x	-	x	x	-	-
10, 10	-	-	-	-	-	-	-	-	-	-
Ace, Ace	x	x	x	x	x	x	x	x	x	-

Example of the schematic representation of the table
Your card values/points > 2 < (4)

Your cards	Bank card									
	2	3	4	5	6	7	8	9	10	Ace
2,2	-	-	**X**	**X**	**X**	**X**	-	-	-	-
3,3	-	-	X	X	X	X	-	-	-	-
4,4	-	-	-	-	-	-	-	-	-	-
5,5	-	-	-	-	-	-	-	-	-	-
6,6	-	X	X	X	X	-	-	-	-	-
7,7	X	X	X	X	X	X	-	-	-	-
8,8	X	X	X	X	X	X	X	X	-	-
9,9	X	X	X	X	X	-	X	X	-	-
10, 10	-	-	-	-	-	-	-	-	-	-
Ace, Ace	X	X	X	X	X	X	X	X	X	-

If your first two cards are 2 and 2 and the bank has a 4 (or even 5, 6, and 7), you should **split**.

If your first two cards are 2 and 2 and the bank has a 2 (or even 3, 8, 9, 10 and Ace), you should **not** split.

Split/Divide: Table structure

The second garage has a glass garage door. Because the glass gate is always stuck, hit it with a heavy sledgehammer every time so that it breaks into a thousand **splinters**.

This glass door garage (second table) contains all card values of the number pictures from light switch (2) to football (11).

This means that the glass door garage (table) is overcrowded and you have to "clean up mentally" there first!

Since you only remember **positive (X)** card combinations, first remove some things from this garage that you don't need in there. These are again the **negative (-)** card combinations, where you remain passive when splitting - as with the previous table.

Imagine that you have to push a **car (4)** with your **hands (5)** through the closed door of the glass garage because there is a **Bible (10)** where the engine normally is.

Your cards	Bank card									
	2	3	4	5	6	7	8	9	10	Ace
2,2	-	-	x	x	x	x	-	-	-	-
3,3	-	-	x	x	x	x	-	-	-	-
4,4 Car	-	-	-	-	-	-	-	-	-	-
5,5 Hand	-	-	-	-	-	-	-	-	-	-
6,6	-	x	x	x	x	-	-	-	-	-
7,7	x	x	x	x	x	x	-	-	-	-
8,8	x	x	x	x	x	x	x	x	-	-
9,9	x	x	x	x	x	-	x	x	-	-
10,10 Bible	-	-	-	-	-	-	-	-	-	-
Ace, Ace	x	x	x	x	x	x	x	x	x	-

**Card values with 4, 5 and 10 points
will not be divided!**

Through your mental cleanup action, the glass door garage is has become much more manageable!

	Your cards	Bank card									
		2	3	4	5	6	7	8	9	10	Ace
1.)	2,2	-	-	x	x	x	x	-	-	-	-
2.)	3,3	-	-	x	x	x	x	-	-	-	-
3.)	6,6	-	x	x	x	x	-	-	-	-	-
4.)	7,7	x	x	x	x	x	x	-	-	-	-
5.)	8,8	x	x	x	x	x	x	x	x	-	-
6.)	9,9	x	x	x	x	x	-	x	x	-	-
7.)	Ace, Ace	x	x	x	x	x	x	x	x	x	-

In order to determine a spatial order - from 1 to 7 - for the glass door garage, please note the following fixed points in a clockwise direction.

1.) At the very front, on the left wall, there is a small **workbench**.
2.) A **wall shelf** hangs above the workbench.
3.) In the middle, on your left garage wall, is a **wooden box**.
4.) On the left side, the head wall, there is a small **upholstered chair**.
5.) There is a **picture** hanging on the right side of the garage head wall.
6.) At the back, on the right wall of the garage, there is a **small table**.
7.) In front, on the right wall, there is a **bucket**.

Annotation:
The "furnishings" in this, the third and fourth "garage" are identical and in the same spatial order.
Please try to imagine/memorize the objects in their arrangement and order as vividly as possible!

Except for the split combination 9.9, for all other combinations, for the sake of simplicity, only remember the front and rear positive (**X**) combinations.

Your cards/points	Bank card									
	2	3	4	5	6	7	8	9	10	Ace
2,2	-	-	**X**	x	x	**X**	-	-	-	-
3,3	-	-	**X**	x	x	**X**	-	-	-	-
6,6	-	**X**	x	x	**X**	-	-	-	-	-
7,7	**X**	x	x	x	x	**X**	-	-	-	-
8,8	**X**	x	x	x	x	x	x	**X**	-	-
9,9	**X**	x	x	x	**X**	-	**X**	**X**	-	-
Ace, Ace	**X**	x	x	x	x	x	x	x	**X**	-

As a reminder:
> The better and more noticeable you are mentally appreciating your pictures and stories
> produce, the better and faster they can be re-produced (remembered) later!

Now imagine that you want to enter your second garage (table/split). Since the glass garage door is stuck again, hit it with the sledgehammer - as usual - so that it shatters into a thousand **splinters**!

Splitting - card combination 2,2

Your cards/points	Bank card									
	2	3	**4**	5	6	**7**	8	9	10	Ace
1.) 2,2 Light switch	-	-	**X Car**	x	x	**X Dwarf**	-	-	-	-

After you have roughly swept away the shards, you enter the glass door garage and painfully hit your left thigh on a small **workbench** (1st spatial order), which is located at the very front of the left wall. As your pain subsides, slowly move your gaze from left to right (clockwise).

First you see that there is a **light switch** (card combination 2,2) on the worktop of the **workbench** (1st spatial order). When you press this, a small toy car appears on the plate (4 = front positive card value). Inside is a small but extremely lively and annoying **dwarf** (7 = rear positive card value), who honks unpleasantly loudly in protest that you have woken him up!

Splitting - card combination 3,3

Your cards/points	Bank card									
	2	3	4	5	6	7	8	9	10	Ace
2.) 3,3 Stool	-	-	**X Car**	x	x	**X Dwarf**	-	-	-	-

Next you will see that there is a **wall shelf** (2nd spatial order) above the workbench. On the shelf there is a small **stool** (card combination 3,3) on which there is another small toy **car** (4 = front positive card value). This is probably controlled by the twin brother of the first **dwarf** (7 = rear positive card value), as he now also joins in the horn concert.

Splitting - card combination 6.6

Your cards/points	Bank card									
	2	3	4	5	6	7	8	9	10	Ace
3.) 6,6 Dice	-	**X**	x	x	**X**	-	-	-	-	-

Third, there is a **wooden box** (3rd spatial order) on the floor approximately in the middle of your left garage wall.
On the box you see an oversized **dice** (card combination 6,6), on the top surface of which a **stool** (3 = front positive card value) is attached upside down and therefore its three legs point upwards. Between the legs of the stool there is a large glass **dice** (6 = rear positive card value) that rotates around its own axis and sparkles strangely.

Splitting - card combination 7,7

Your cards/points	Bank card									
	2	3	4	5	6	7	8	9	10	Ace
4.) 7,7	X	x	x	x	x	X	-	-	-	-

Fourthly, you will see a small **upholstered chair** (4th spatial order) on the left side of the garage head wall.
A large glass garden **gnome** sits on this armchair (card combination 7.7). The garden gnome has a **light switch** where the bulbous nose is usually located (2 = front positive card value). When you press the gnome's nose light switch, there is a shrill sound and suddenly another garden **gnome** (7 = rear positive card value) is sitting next to the first one!

Splitting - card combination 8,8

Your cards/points	Bank card									
	2	3	4	5	6	7	8	9	10	Ace
5.) 8,8	X	x	x	x	x	x	x	X	-	-

Fifthly, on the right side of the garage head wall you will see a **picture** (5th spatial order) on which a **roller coaster** (card combination 8.8) is painted.
The roller coaster cars look like oversized **light switches** (2 = front positive card value).
A small **cat** (7 = rear positive card value) sits in one of the cars and goes for a drive.

Splitting - card combination 9,9

Your cards/points	Bank card									
	2	3	4	5	6	7	8	9	10	Ace
6.) 9,9	X	x	x	x	X	-	X	X	-	-

The sixth item you will see at the back of the right garage wall is a small **table** (6th spatial order), which has two drawers below the table top.
There is a tiger (cat, card combination 9.9) sitting under the table, guarding the **light switch** in the left drawer (2 = first front positive card value) and the **dice** (6 = first rear positive card value) in the right drawer.

On the table you see a small **roller coaster** (8 = second front positive card value) with which a small tiger **cat** baby (9 = second rear positive card value) rides through the curves meowing loudly.

Splitting - card combination As, As

Your cards/points	Bank card									
	2	3	4	5	6	7	8	9	10	Ace
7.) As, As	X	x	x	x	x	x	x	x	X	-

As the seventh and final "furnishing item" in your glass door garage, you will see a **bucket** (7th spatial order) on the front right side of the garage wall in which there is a **soccer ball** (card combination As, As = 11).
There is a **light switch** on this ball (2 = front positive card value) which, when activated, turns the ball into a **Bible** (11 = rear positive card value).

Summary - Splitting

Your cards/points	Bank card									
	2	3	4	5	6	7	8	9	10	Ace
1.) Workbench 2,2	-	-	X	x	x	X	-	-	-	-
2.) Wall shelf 3,3	-	-	X	x	x	X	-	-	-	-
3.) Wooden box 6,6	-	X	x	x	X	-	-	-	-	-
4.) Upholstered chair 7,7	X	x	x	x	x	X	-	-	-	-
5.) Picture 8,8	X	x	x	x	x	x	x	X	-	-
6.) Table 9,9	X	x	x	x	X	-	X	X	-	-
7.) Bucket Ace, Ace	X	x	x	x	x	x	x	x	X	-

Gray background = Become positive/active and split

Just memorize the fields marked in gray (X)

White = Stay negative/passive, don't split

Please summarize the spatial order, stories and numerical images in your glass door garage one or more times mentally and with a lot of imagination.

Take playing cards/buy cards
The basic rules again in brief

In the game of Black Jack, each card represents a certain point value.

Counting aces (player's choice)
either 11 points or 1 point.

Pictures (Jacks, Queens and Kings) count 10 points. All other cards count the printed point value.
The aim of the game is for you to use your cards to gain a point or hand advantage over the bank without buying too many playing cards.

Each player is dealt two cards face up by the dealer/croupier. The bank receives one card face up and one face down. After dealing cards, you decide whether you want to buy more cards or not.
The dealer/croupier must buy up to 16 points and is not allowed to buy any more cards after 17 points. In contrast to the dealer/croupier, the player is allowed to buy additional cards or fold with each score.

Hard hand
If you don't have an ace or have an ace that only counts for 1 point because you would otherwise get over 21 points, you have what is called a "hard hand".

Examples:
If you have a 7, a 5, and a 4, hold one:
"Hard hand 16".
If you have an 8, a 6, and an Ace, hold one:
"Hard hand 15".

Soft hand
If you have an ace that still counts for 11 points, you are holding a so-called "Soft hand".

Example:
If you have an Ace and a 5, you hold a "Soft hand 16"

> When and whether you should buy more cards doesn't just depend on yours score, but also on whether you have one
> Hold a "hard hand" or a "soft hand".

Hard hand

The table below shows which card combinations you should buy in a "hard hand" (**X**) and when not (-).

Your cards/points	Bank card									
	2	3	4	5	6	7	8	9	10	Ace
11	If there are fewer than 12 points, you always buy									
12	x	x	-	-	-	x	x	x	x	x
13	-	-	-	-	-	x	x	x	x	x
14	-	-	-	-	-	x	x	x	x	x
15	-	-	-	-	-	x	x	x	x	x
16	-	-	-	-	-	x	x	x	x	x
17	-	-	-	-	-	-	-	-	-	-
18	-	-	-	-	-	-	-	-	-	-
19	-	-	-	-	-	-	-	-	-	-

Scores 17 and 18 depend on
whether you "count" cards or not.

If you have more than 18 points you will never buy!

Example of the schematic representation of the table
Your card values/points > 12 <

Your cards/points	Bank card									
	2	3	4	5	6	7	8	9	10	Ace
12	x	x	-	-	-	x	x	x	x	x

If you have a 5 and a 7 (hard hand 12) and the bank has a 2 (or 3, 7, 8, 9, 10, Ace), then you should buy cards.

If you have a 9 and a 3 (hard hand 12) and the bank has a 4 (or 5, 6), then you should not buy.

As a reminder:
Garage door number 3 is very valuable because it is covered in diamonds. Diamond is the hardest (**Hard**-hand) material on earth. The diamond gate garage (third table) contains the point values from 11 to 19 (left column, your cards).
This means that the diamond gate garage (table) is also overcrowded and you should mentally tidy up here too!
That you should buy cards under 12 points and over 16 points only as a card counter, can you easily remember:
Imagine that on the roof of the diamond gate garage a ghost (12) is dancing with a young pretty **girl** (16, teenager) and you know which **scores** are summarized in this third table.

Your cards/points	Bank card									
	2	3	4	5	6	7	8	9	10	Ace
Ghost 12	x	x	-	-	-	x	x	x	x	x
13	-	-	-	-	-	x	x	x	x	x
14	-	-	-	-	-	x	x	x	x	x
15	-	-	-	-	-	x	x	x	x	x
Teenager 16	-	-	-	-	-	x	x	x	x	x

As a reminder:
The third and fourth garages are "set up" just like the second!

1.) At the very front, on the left wall, there is a small workbench.
2.) A wall shelf hangs above the workbench.
3.) In the middle, on your left garage wall, is a wooden box.
4.) On the left side, the head wall, there is a small upholstered chair.
5.) There is a picture hanging on the right side of the garage head wall.
6.) At the back, on the right wall of the garage, there is a small table.
7.) In front, on the right wall, there is a bucket.

Except for the score **12**, for all other combinations, for the sake of simplicity, again only remember the front and back positive (**X**) combinations.

Hard hand – 12 Points

Your cards/points	Bank card									
	2	3	4	5	6	7	8	9	10	Ace
1.) Ghost **12**	X	X	-	-	-	X	x	x	x	X

You now open the gate of your diamond gate garage, which sparkles wonderfully in the sunlight, and let your gaze slowly wander from left to right (clockwise).
At the very front on the left wall, under the workbench (1st spatial order), you can see the dancing ghost from the roof (12 = total number of points for your first two cards), which now guards the contents of the two drawers below the workbench top. In the left drawer there is a light switch (2 = first front positive card value) and in the right drawer there is a small diamond-studded stool (3 = first back positive card value).

On the workbench you will see an extremely aggressive **dwarf** (7 = second front positive card value) who is throwing **soccer balls** (11 = second back positive card value) at you.

Please let your imagination run wild!

Hard hand – 13 Points

Your cards/points	Bank card									
	2	3	4	5	6	7	8	9	10	Ace
2.) Elevator **13**	-	-	-	-	-	**X**	x	x	x	**X**

For example, on the wall shelf (2nd spatial order) above the workbench you could see a miniature **elevator** (13 = total number of points of your first two cards), in which the sliding door now opens and another **dwarf** (7 = front positive card value) Throws a **soccer ball** at her (11 = rear positive card value).

> ## The front and rear positive card value is from the Score/column 13 to 16 always the same...

...so that you only need to remember the dwarf - who throws footballs at you, or juggles with them, etc. - as the front and back card values. Regardless, I would also like to present you with some short stories for the following table columns.

♠

Hard hand – 14 Points

Your cards/points	Bank card									
	2	3	4	5	6	7	8	9	10	Ace
3.) Heart **14**	-	-	-	-	-	**X**	x	x	x	**X**

In the middle of your left garage wall, on the **wooden box** (3rd spatial order), there is a small red **heart**-shaped bed studded with diamonds (14 = total number of points of your first two cards), on which another poison **dwarf** (7) stands and you also have **soccer balls** (11) is thrown at.

Hard hand – 15 Points

Your cards/points	Bank card									
	2	3	4	5	6	7	8	9	10	Ace
4.) Knight **15**	-	-	-	-	-	**X**	x	x	x	**X**

On the left side of the garage head wall there is an upholstered chair (4th spatial order). On this sits a militant **dwarf** dressed as a **knight** (15 = total points of your first two cards) who even shoots **footballs** at you from a cannon!

Hard hand – 16 Points

Your cards/points	Bank card									
	2	3	4	5	6	7	8	9	10	Ace
5.) Teenager **16**	-	-	-	-	-	**X**	x	x	x	**X**

Lastly - excluding the card counter - you will see a picture (5th spatial order) in your diamond gate garage on the right side of the garage head wall, with a young, **pretty girl** standing on its wide picture frame (16 teenagers = total number of points for your first two cards) and throws throwing material in the form of **footballs** at the **dwarves**.

Hard hand - Summary

Your cards/points		Bank card									
		2	3	4	5	6	7	8	9	10	Ace
1.) Ghost	12	X	X	-	-	-	X	x	x	x	X
2.) Elvator	13	-	-	-	-	-	X	x	x	x	X
3.) Heart	14	-	-	-	-	-	X	x	x	x	X
4.) Knight	15	-	-	-	-	-	X	x	x	x	X
5.) Teenager	16	-	-	-	-	-	X	x	x	x	X

Gray background = Be positive/active and buy cards

Only note the fields highlighted in gray (X)

White = Stay negative/passive, don't buy

Please summarize the spatial order, stories and numerical images in your diamond gate garage one or more times mentally and with a lot of imagination.

Soft hand

If you have an Ace that still counts for 11 points, you are holding a so-called "**soft hand**".
The table for buying cards with a soft hand is completely different than that for buying with a hard hand.
The table below shows which card combinations you should buy in a "soft hand" (**X**) and when not (-).

Your cards/points	Bank card									
	2	3	4	5	6	7	8	9	10	Ace
Ace + 2 = **13**	x	x	x	x	x	x	x	x	x	x
Ace + 3 = **14**	x	x	x	x	x	x	x	x	x	x
Ace + 4 = **15**	x	x	x	x	x	x	x	x	x	x
Ace + 5 = **16**	x	x	x	x	x	x	x	x	x	x
Ace + 6 = **17**	x	x	x	x	x	x	x	x	x	x
Ace + 7 = **18**	-	-	-	-	-	-	-	x	x	x
Ace + 8 = **19**	-	-	-	-	-	-	-	-	-	-
Ace + 9 = **20**	-	-	-	-	-	-	-	-	-	-

As a reminder:
The fourth and final garage does not have a garage door! Instead, there is an oversized soft ice cream machine that you have to laboriously push aside every time you want to get in.

With this table, you only remember the front and back positive (X) card combinations.
First, initiate a "mental clean-up" here too:
Remember the upper and lower total points from Soft hand 13 to Soft hand 18 by imagining an **elevator** (= 13) on the roof of your soft ice cream machine garage, with a large **cloud** (stands for after-work traffic = 18) of car exhaust coming out of the door exit.

Table after the "mental cleanup"

Your cards/points	Bank card									
	2	3	4	5	6	7	8	9	10	Ace
Ace + 2 = **13** **Elevator**	**X**	x	x	x	x	x	x	x	x	**X**
Ace + **3**	**X**	x	x	x	x	x	x	x	x	**X**
Ace + **4**	**X**	x	x	x	x	x	x	x	x	**X**
Ace + **5**	**X**	x	x	x	x	x	x	x	x	**X**
Ace + **6**	**X**	x	x	x	x	x	x	x	x	**X**
Ace + 7 = **18** **Closing time**	-	-	-	-	-	-	-	**X**	x	**X**

Soft hand – 13 Points

Your cards/points	Bank card									
	2	3	4	5	6	7	8	9	10	Ace
Ace + 2 = **13** 1.) **Elevator**	**X**	x	x	x	x	x	x	x	x	**X**

When you let your gaze wander from left to right again, you see a small **elevator** (Soft hand 13) on the **workbench** top (1st spatial order).
Inside the elevator there is an oversized light switch (2 = front positive card value). When you press the light switch, there is an explosion and the elevator turns into a huge football (11 = rear positive card value).

Soft hand – 14 Points

Your cards/points	Bank card									
	2	3	4	5	6	7	8	9	10	Ace
Ace + 3 = **14** 2.) **Heart**	**X**	x	x	x	x	x	x	x	x	**X**

On the **wall shelf** (2nd spatial order), above the workbench, you will see a large gingerbread **heart** (Soft hand 14). In the middle there is a **light switch** (front positive card value). When you press this too, the same thing happens that happened before with the elevator. There is a detonation and the gingerbread heart turns into a voluminous **football** (rear positive card value).

Soft hand – 15 Points

Your cards/points	Bank card									
	2	3	4	5	6	7	8	9	10	Ace
Ace + 4 = **15** 3.) **Knight**	**X**	x	x	x	x	x	x	x	x	**X**

On the **wooden box** (3rd spatial order) sits a **knight** (soft hand 15) who has a **light switch** (front positive card value) on his breastplate. You press it, a clap of thunder and the knight is enchanted into a **football** (rear positive card value).

Soft hand – 16 Points

Your cards/points	Bank card									
	2	3	4	5	6	7	8	9	10	Ace
Ace + 5 = 16 4.) **Teenager**	**X**	x	x	x	x	x	x	x	x	**X**

A **teenager** (soft hand 16) is sitting on the **upholstered chair** (4th spatial order) on the garage head wall and is holding out a **light switch** to you with both hands. It's a shame for the teenager, who now also says good-bye with a loud bang and turns into a **soccer ball**.

Soft hand – 17 Points

Your cards/points	Bank card									
	2	3	4	5	6	7	8	9	10	Ace
Ace + 6 = 17 5.) **Card game**	**X**	x	x	x	x	x	x	x	x	**X**

On the right side of the garage head wall there is an **oil painting** (5th spatial order) depicting a **card player** (soft hand 17) at the black jack table. However, there are no playing cards on the Black Jack table, just many small **light switches** that, at the push of a button, enchant the card player into a **football**!

Soft hand – 18 Points

Your cards/points	Bank card									
	2	3	4	5	6	7	8	9	10	Ace
Ace + 7 = **18** 6.) **Closing time**	-	-	-	-	-	-	-	**X**	x	**X**

The last thing you see on the **table** (6th spatial order), on the right-hand garage wall, is a **traffic sign** (stands for After work - traffic, Soft hand 18) on which a small **cat** is playing **football**.

Soft hand – summary

Your cards/points	Bank card									
	2	3	4	5	6	7	8	9	10	Ace
Ace + **2** Elevator = 13	**X**	x	x	x	x	x	x	x	x	**X**
Ace + **3** Heart = 14	**X**	x	x	x	x	x	x	x	x	**X**
Ace + **4** Knight = 15	**X**	x	x	x	x	x	x	x	x	**X**
Ace + **5** Teenager = 16	**X**	x	x	x	x	x	x	x	x	**X**
Ace + **6** Card game = 17	**X**	x	x	x	x	x	x	x	x	**X**
Ace + **7** Closing time = 18	-	-	-	-	-	-	-	**X**	x	**X**

Before you continue reading, please make sure to mentally consolidate all 4 tables. The cheapest and fastest way to achieve this is, for example, to download Black Jack simulation software from the Internet.

Your basic strategy

The 4 tables, which you can now safely recall from memory, are referred to as the basic strategy for a professional Black Jack game. With this strategy, the player makes his decisions solely depending on the bank's face-up card and his own cards.

Unless you play Black Jack machines or in a casino with shuffling machines, you can expand this basic strategy to create an even more efficient game of Black Jack by including the recording and evaluation of the cards that have already been played.

A detailed description of this technology can be found on the following pages.

Card counting

Recommendation:

Never use words like: card counting, count or similar in a casino or to your fellow players. Avoid anything that could in any way indicate that you have mastered or used this technique.

Always behave as inconspicuously as possible!

Therefore, never use terms such as basic, stand, hit, bust, etc. in a German-speaking casino.

What is card counting?

When playing the lottery, roulette or dice, etc., the frequency or number of numbers already drawn or dropped does not affect the sequence or probability of future numbers!

For example, if the number 13 is drawn five times in a row in the lottery, this does not in any way increase or decrease the probability that this number will be drawn again in the next draw - because this number was/will be drawn at random!

This is also the reason why there cannot be any effective systems for such games.

In a card game, however, the remaining cards are directly dependent on the cards already drawn!

For example, if you draw an Ace of Hearts as the top card of a Black Jack game and put it aside, you know with one hundred percent that the remaining 51 cards will not contain any more Ace of Hearts.

At the same time, your chance of drawing an Ace of Clubs as your next card has increased from 1:52 to 1:51.

When playing Black Jack, it is a huge advantage for you if you know which cards have already been drawn.

Here too, you can literally bene**fit** from your knowledge from the first chapter!

However, if you skipped the first chapter, you will have difficulty memorizing, for example, 100 playing cards in the order.

Nevertheless, you can learn a simplified card memorization technique using so-called "card counting" by dividing the 52 different playing cards into three categories, for example:

First: "Small cards" with point values of 2, 3, 4, 5 and 6
Second: "Medium cards" with point values from 7 to 9
Third: "Big cards" with point values from 10 to 11

Since the bank has to buy cards up to 16 points, it is an advantage for the bank if there are as many "small cards" such as 2, 3, 4, 5 and 6 in the game (deck) as possible! This reduces the bank's risk of overbuying.

For you as a player, however, it is an advantage if there are more "big cards" such as 10, pictures or aces still in play!

For two reasons:

Firstly, the probability of Black Jack increases, which gives you as a player a winning ratio of 3:2 and for the bank only a win equal to the player's stake.

Second, the bank overbuys more often because the bank has to buy until 16, while you can buy as many or as few cards as you wish.

The combination of basic and card counting strategy is what makes Black Jack the only casino game that gives the player a real advantage over the bank.

Card counting - theory and practice

The technique and theory of card counting is relatively quick and easy to learn.

The difficulty lies in the practical application, as the game requires you to concentrate on several things at the same time.

This means that you not only have to concentrate on counting your own cards, but also those of your fellow players and the croupier.

Furthermore, you must simultaneously concentrate on your basic strategy as well as on the conversation with the croupier and your fellow players. In addition, you will almost always encounter other unforeseeable influences during the course of a deck, which are not exactly conducive to optimal concentration. For example, if you are approached from behind asking if you would like something more to drink, etc.

Suddenly you no longer know where you stopped counting and your entire deck is "broken"!

For this reason, I will first describe the basic technique to you and then introduce a special memorization technique that you can use to be successful in practical application.

Counting cards - basic technique
Example using a simple deck with 52 cards (running count).

As mentioned at the beginning, it is an advantage for the bank if there are as many "small cards" such as 2, 3, 4, 5 and 6 in the deck!

For you as a player, however, it is an advantage if more "big cards" such as 10, Jack, Queen, King or Ace are still in play!

The "middle cards" with point values of 7 to 9 bring neither you nor the bank any particular advantages or disadvantages and are therefore to be viewed as neutral.

Das bedeutet:

A complete deck contains 20 particularly positive and 12 neutral cards for both you and the bank.

The deck is therefore evenly balanced for both parties.

If the first cards have been drawn and there are, for example, 10 "small cards" but only 5 "big cards" left, the chances - as far as the remaining cards are concerned - are no longer balanced.

In this case, there are only 10 cards left in the deck for the bank, but 15 particularly positive cards for you! So you literally have "the better cards" for the rest of the deck.

It is obvious that if you have such an advantage, you should increase your stake or adjust your basic strategy.

I will address this topic separately later.

To determine the proportion of positive or negative cards in the remaining deck for you, you have to "count" them!

When counting cards, start at 0 (zero) because the positive/negative cards are balanced in a deck that is still complete.
You mentally add a plus sign (+) to the cards that are positive for the bank when they are drawn - because it is a plus (+) for you - when these cards are no longer in the deck.

You count cards from 2 to 6 as +1

You mentally add a minus sign (-) to the cards that are positive for you, 10, Jack, Queen, King and Ace, when they are drawn - because it is a minus (-) for you - if these cards are no longer in the deck.

Count the cards from 10 to 11 as -1

Count the neutral cards from 7 to 9 as 0 or not

Example of the first 10 cards

Cards	Jack	2	8	4	3	Ace	10	Queen	King	10
Counter	- 1	+ 1	0	+1	+1	- 1	- 1	- 1	- 1	- 1

Result: - 3

This result is not particularly favorable for you and you should be cautious about the size of your stakes the next time you play.
We continue with the cards from 11 to 20:
You start counting with -3 as the following cards are dealt from the same/previous deck (first 10 cards above).

Weitere 10 Karten

Cards	4	2	6	Jack	3	Ace	9	5	5	6
Counter	+ 1	+ 1	+1	- 1	+1	- 1	0	+ 1	+ 1	+ 1

Overall result after the first 20 cards: + 2

This result is favorable for you and you now have a slight advantage over the bank.
In order to be able to use the card counting technique practically, you need to practice it! To do this, take a complete deck of 52 cards.

Now slowly count through the entire deck using the procedure described. When you turn over the last card, you should be back to a neutral value:

(0)

Otherwise you have miscounted!

Make your exercises a little more difficult from time to time, for example by having a radio playing in the background. Later, count the cards while watching TV and/or talking to someone.
Practice until you can count really quickly and effortlessly, and keep repeating your basic strategies before coming back here.

Card counting - brain-friendly

Have you now practiced card counting and noticed that you had a little blackout more or less often?!
Maybe you were distracted by little things - like the phone ringing - or you simply forgot whether your last count was a +1 or -1, etc.?!
As mentioned at the beginning, numbers are only digital and therefore abstract information for our brain.

Furthermore, you have now convinced yourself that you can memorize/recall digital information such as tables etc. much better and faster if you visualize it and structure it in a brain-friendly way!

You can now also benefit from the tree list (or a list from the first chapter) that you have developed for this purpose when counting cards.
In order not to confuse +1 with -1 in the future, you will restructure your counting method using the tree list.
As a rule, the count values vary between + 9 and - 9.
With regard to the tree list, you could also say from 1 (tree) to 18 (closing time), or to 19 (dinner), if you include 0 (neutral cards) as a "value"!
The lack of plus and minus signs not only makes counting easier, but also eliminates the possibility of confusing +/-.

Take a look at the modified tree list below for a few minutes and make up your own mind before reading further.

The number pictures – list
for card counting

Count value	Minus, neutral and plus cards
1. Tree	- 9
2. Light switch	- 8
3. Stool	- 7
4. Car	- 6
5. Hand	- 5
6. Dice	- 4
7. Dwarf	- 3
8. Roller coaster	- 2
9. Cat	**- 1 = For "large cards" 10 to 11 points**
10. Bible	**0 = For "neutral cards" 7 to 9 points**
11. Football	**+ 1 = For "small cards" 2 to 6 points**
12. Ghost	+ 2
13. Elevator	+ 3
14. Heart	+ 4
15. Knight	+ 5
16. Teenager	+ 6
17. Card game	+ 7
18. Closing time	+ 8
19. Dinner	+ 9
20. TV news	+ 10

Surely you figured it out yourself?!

With this type of card counting - count in pictures!

Instead of 0, start with the Bible when the first card should be a neutral 7, 8 or 9.

You have already stored the "counting pictures" in your subconscious when you learned your basic strategy and are therefore easier to remember than digital information such as numbers. Furthermore, the risk of confusing plus and minus numbers and vice versa is virtually eliminated.

Now mentally count the cards that are positive for the bank, as with the basic technique, in the upper plus range (+) from football (11) to dinner (19), since it is a plus (+) for you if these cards are - As the game progresses - it is no longer in the deck.

Mentally count the cards that are positive for you, 10, Jack, Queen, King and Ace, in the negative range (-) from cat to tree, because it will be a minus (-) for you - as the game progresses - if these cards are no longer in the cards deck.

Example of the first 10 cards

Original counting method

Cards	Jack	2	8	4	3	Ace	10	Queen	King	10
Zähler	- 1	+ 1	0	+1	+1	- 1	- 1	- 1	- 1	- 1

Counting cards with counting pictures – MLS - BJ*

Cards	Jack	2	8	4	3
Counter 0	9 Cat	10 Bible	10 Bible	11 Soccer	12 Ghost
	- 1	+ 1	0	+1	+1

Cards	Ace	10	Queen	King	10
Counter 0	11 Soccerl	10 Bible	9 Cat	Roller coaster	Dwarf
	- 1	- 1	- 1	- 1	- 1

Result: 7 dwarf (- 3)

Now please imagine - as imaginatively as possible - a little dwarf on your left shoe who is making faces at you while laughing.

* MLS – BJ = Michael Lutz System – Black Jack

When you see this image crystal clear in your mind's eye, stop your exercises for 10 to 20 minutes and do something completely different.

With the short interruption you have simulated a situation that could also happen to you at the gaming table. For example, if, out of the blue, the person sitting next to you asks you about your great jacket and he really wants the name, address and telephone number of your tailor!
In this case, the person sitting next to you at the table would have the correct multi-digit phone number for your tailor, but you (as a beginner with the traditional card counting method) would most likely not remember the single-digit count at which you were interrupted.
But if I ask you what you "saw" on your left shoe/foot before your break, you probably won't have any trouble remembering the little dwarf who made faces at you while laughing out loud.
The dwarf (- 3) was your last counting picture and you could remember it so easily (brain-friendly) because the digital information (- 3) is not only illustrated (dwarf), but also like on your computer in a folder (on your shoe).

They had assigned the dwarf a permanent place,
to be sure to find this information again!

Just like you have a fixed place for your front door key - the key box - so you don't have to constantly look for it!

Since your shoe would quickly be overfilled with gnomes, roller coasters and ghosts etc. during a Black Jack session lasting several hours, you need a fixed "list" with at least 10 locations structured in their order.
In the first chapter you will find numerous examples of how you can create such folders and watch lists. If you skipped Chapter 1, I would like to briefly introduce or remind you of two of these lists.

Please remember what I already pointed out to you at the beginning of Chapter 2:

Try to implement the exercises "1 to 1" if possible.
It works!

To stick with your shoe/foot, start your first exercise with the "**body list**."

Recommendation:
Before you start the exercises, read the entire process below at least once so that you can carry out the exercises one after the other and coherently.
If you have any physical problems (please only then), you can do the exercises sitting or mentally.

Body list - order from bottom to top

First, please stand upright, bend your torso and touch your shoes/feet with both hands and say loudly:

My foot is number 1 on my body list
Then touch your kneecaps with your hands:
Knee is number 2
Now grab your thighs and say:
Thigh - 3
Touch your buttocks cheeks with both hands:
Buttocks - 4
Next, touch your hip and say out loud again:
My hip is number 5
Now place both hands on your chest and shout:
The chest is the 6th
With both arms crossed, grab your shoulders:
Shoulder - 7
Put your hands on your neck and say:
Neck is 8
Touch your nose, press it a little and say nasally:
The nose is 9
Lastly, touch the top half of your head/hair:
My hair is number 10 on my body list

The body list should literally become "flesh and blood" to you. Even if this list seems very simple to you, please practice it until you can recite it backwards and "mixed" without thinking.

Location list - order from left to right

Another option is, for example, to create a watch list of the place where you are currently.
You proceed in roughly the same way as you mentally "set up" the "garages" with the workbench, the wall shelf, the wooden box, etc. in your order (clockwise).
Suppose you are sitting at the gaming table in a casino and let your gaze (real this time) move from left to right.
The first object you might see is a clothes rack, the second object a roulette table, etc.; then remember these objects until you have set a total of 10 fixed points as your personal memory locations.
Place your counting pictures on these fixed points one after the other - in the order from left to right - as you noted the dwarf (-3) on your shoes.
The location list has the advantage that it can be remembered and recalled very quickly because you can see the things and objects in their order.
You could then have imagined and remembered the dwarf on your place list, for example on the clothes rack (1st position on the place list).
Feel free to practice these lists in a context other than Black Jack.
For example, try to place your next shopping list on the body list by placing the eggs you want to buy in your shoes as imaginatively as possible and linking the butter to your knee accordingly, etc.!

We continue with the cards from 11 to 20

You start counting again with the Dwarf (-3), on your first body list position (the shoe), as the following cards are dealt from the same deck (first 10 cards).

Original counting method – Starting at - 3

Cards	4	2	6	Jack	3	Ace	9	5	5	6
Counter	+ 1	+ 1	+1	- 1	+1	- 1	0	+ 1	+ 1	+ 1

Counting cards with counting pictures -MLS-BJ- Starting at 7 Dwarf

Cards	4	2	6	Jack	3
Counter	8 Roller coaster	9 Cat	10 Bible	9 Cat	10 Bible
- 3	+ 1	+ 1	+ 1	- 1	+1

Cards	Ace	9	5	5	6
Counter	9 Cat	9 Cat	10 Bible	11 Soccer	12 Ghost
0	- 1	0	+ 1	+ 1	+ 1

Overall result after 20 cards: 12 Ghost (+ 2)

If the person sitting next to you at the table asks you for your wife's cell phone number, mentally link the **ghost** with your **knee** (2nd position on the body list) and you will later know at which count value you have to continue!

The counting pictures not only have the advantage that they are easier to remember, but also save you the trouble of calculating. You can also compare this list to a ladder.

The higher you climb, the higher your chances are!

Counting without numbers

This type of card counting will be a little difficult for you at first. Before using it in practice, you should practice this technique until you believe you can use it safely and quickly. To do this, take a complete deck of 52 cards. Now count the entire deck slowly using your number pictures using the procedure described at the beginning.

When you turn over the last card, you must be back to the neutral value 0 (the Bible).

Make your exercises a little more difficult from time to time. For example, listen to some music or watch a movie on TV at the same time - while you count. Then later, count cards while talking to someone. When you think you have mastered the counting technique, you can start by turning 2 cards at a time. To better control the accuracy of your counting results, you should put several decks of cards together and count them.

As already mentioned, you can download free Black Jack games from the Internet to practice. The programs allow you to play with up to 5 players at the same time, which is quite close to reality, as in practice you also have to count the cards of your fellow players.

In these simulated games, card counting obviously has no effect on your chances of winning because the cards are shuffled using a random generator, like in a slot machine. Nevertheless, these digital games are an excellent and, above all, free training to prepare for the first practical test in the casino.

Practice until you can count really quickly and effortlessly and recall your basic strategy. Please only continue reading here if you think you are prepared for the first practical test.

How you benefit from card counting*

The greater the difference between the counting pictures and the "Bible" (neutral value), the more you should adapt your stake and also your basic strategy to the respective game situation!

Positive count value
In a deck with a predominantly positive (+) count, there are more large cards than small cards.
As a result, you will also draw more large cards than small cards from the remaining deck.
In this situation you can risk doubling your usual stake from a count of 13 elevator (+3) and with 16 teenager (+6) you could well dare to even quadruple your usual stake.
Of course, with such a positive count as teenagers, you should also rethink and adapt your basic strategy.
If the bank holds a 9 or 10 and your first two cards total 15 or 16 points, you should not buy another card (contrary to your basic strategy).
The chances of you overbuying are too high.

Negative count value
This is different with a deck with a predominantly negative (-) count.
If there are more small cards than large cards in the rest of the deck, you will of course - in the order of play - receive more small cards than large cards.
In this situation, you are at a disadvantage compared to the bank and you should keep your stakes to a minimum, but you should also not skip your bets every time, as you could very quickly be exposed as a "professional".
From a negative count like Dwarf (-3) you should also correct your basic strategy.
If the bank holds a 4, 5 or 6 and your first two cards total 12 points, you should draw another card.

---

*The following deployment and strategy variations, with changing counts, are not exact calculations, but merely examples to explain the principle!

If the bank holds a 2 and you have 13 points, buy one more card. If the count is very negative, you should not only hold back on your bets, but also when doubling, as you will only receive one more card after doubling.

Stop doubling at 10 vs. 9.

When splitting, however, you can use your basic strategy regardless of the count value.

Behave inconspicuously

No matter how well you master basic strategy and card counting, you will still have days where you will mostly lose. Especially if you are a beginner, you should be cautious about the size of your stakes. As already mentioned, you cannot count cards at slot machines or in casinos with shuffling machines. In this case, you have to limit yourself to your basic strategy. If the table is shuffled by hand and counted by you, you should never play for more than an hour at a time. The risk that you will be "seen through" as a counter increases with every minute.

A final and very personal recommendation...

During my research I was lucky enough to meet a proven Black Jack expert (he read this book):

Graduate economist **Horst Behrend**. The "Black Jack Professor", known for his numerous press and television appearances, lives in Palma de Mallorca, where he instructs beginners and advanced players in the game of Black Jack in one-day individual seminars.

...and another request on my own behalf:

This book has been translated from German into English for the first time as a new edition. If you discover any errors or have suggestions for a better or clearer translation, I would be very grateful for your feedback.

And... I'm currently working on a continuation of the "The perfect memory training not just for card players" series on the subject of poker.

Here too, I would be very happy to hear your ideas and suggestions!

Contact: **lutz@genialgemerkt.de**

I wish you a lot of fun and success with the exercises and the use of the card memory techniques and hope that you will benefit from this book in many ways!

To you - always a good hand, good luck and of course always a winning *Black Jack without a black out!*

Until then, I wish you all the best, *Michael Lutz*

Recommendation and notice

This book is also available in a hardcover gift edition, as well as an abridged edition, consisting of the first chapter of this book entitled "Memorize playing cards in seconds" with the subtitle "The perfect memory training not just for card players"

1530.

Wappen-Familie
der
Sutz.

Notes

Notes